SUPERCOP NSA

AJIT DOVAL

SUPERCOP NSA
AJIT DOVAL

MAHESH DUTT SHARMA

PRABHAT PRAKASHAN

Published by
PRABHAT PRAKASHAN PVT. LTD.
4/19 Asaf Ali Road,
New Delhi-110 002 (INDIA)
e-mail: prabhatbooks@gmail.com

ISBN 978-93-5521-129-3
SUPERCOP NSA AJIT DOVAL
by Mahesh Dutt Sharma

Edition
2026

Price
₹ 400 (Rupees Four Hundred Only)

Printed at
R-Tech Offset Printers, Delhi

Author's Note

Ajit Doval is one of the most respected officers of the Indian Police Service. He is the first police officer to receive the 'Kirti Chakra' which is the second-highest gallantry award after the 'Param Vir Chakra'. He joined the IPS in 1968 in the Kerala cadre and retired in January 2005 as the director of the Intelligence Bureau.

Hailing from Garhwal, Doval has excellent credentials as 'Operation Man'. He made a name for himself as a field operative during the Mizoram rebellion, where he overpowered the rebel leader, Laldenga. In 1989, he led an Intelligence Bureau (IB) team with the Punjab Police and the National Security Guard during 'Operation Black Thunder' to flush out terrorists from the Golden Temple in Amritsar.

Throughout the years, he headed several important teams within the IB, including those with prominent operations against Islamic terrorism in India. He also led the team formed after the 1993 Mumbai blasts to apprehend underworld gangster Dawood Ibrahim.

He has also served in Pakistan when J.N. Dixit was the High Commissioner of India. He was one of the three interlocutors with diplomat Vivek Katju and Research and Analysis Wing (RAW) intelligence officer C.D. Sahai, who carried out negotiations for the release of the passengers aboard flight IC 814, which had been hijacked to Kandahar.

He has to his credit, dozens of bold campaigns like surgical strikes, the Doklam controversy, controlling the situation in Kashmir after the abrogation of Article 370, military operations in Myanmar, etc. This book presents an interesting story of his life and adventures. It is not only inspiring, it is full of thrilling incidents as well.

—Mahesh Dutt Sharma

Contents

1

Ajit Doval: Introduction to his Life and Career

You must have heard or read about many such brave personalities who went beyond their call of duty to uphold the self-respect and pride of the country. There are many such heroes in India, too, who are always prepared to do anything for the country. One such person is India's National Security Adviser Ajit Doval, whose love for the country knows no bounds. For this very love for the nation, he crossed the border and lived in Pakistan as a spy for almost seven years.

Ajit Doval is a name that needs no introduction today. At present, if someone is called the 'James Bond' of India, then Ajit Doval's name will be the first to come to mind.

Ajit Doval has protected the country's security, at times as a spy and sometimes by disguising himself as a beggar. On account of his unique diplomacy and unmatched strategies, he is called the 'Modern James Bond of India' as well as 'Chanakya'.

Few people know that the national security adviser was an undercover agent in Pakistan.

India's National Security Adviser Ajit Doval is considered to be a specially trusted officer by Prime Minister Narendra Modi.

Ajit Doval, the fifth national security adviser of India and the chairman of the National Security Council, is considered a very powerful person in the central government of the country. He is said to take any decision only after careful consideration and he sticks to it once it is taken.

Born in 1945 in a Garhwali family of Pauri Garhwal, Ajit Doval was a 1968 batch IPS officer of the Kerala cadre. He has been the head of several important departments including the IB. He retired from the post of director of IB in 2005.

'Kirti Chakra' Award

An Indian who does not hesitate to openly warn Pakistan about snatching Balochistan to avenge Mumbai; a spy who was committed to protecting his country by living as a Muslim in Lahore, Pakistan for 7 years.

Ajit Doval is the only citizen of India who has been awarded the Kirti Chakra, the second-highest peacetime award. Originally from Pauri Garhwal, Uttarakhand, Ajit Doval studied at Ajmer Military School and did his MA in economics from Agra University.

Ajit started preparing for the IPS during his postgraduation. With his perseverance, he was selected for the IPS in 1968 from the Kerala cadre.

National Security Adviser

Ajit Doval is a retired IPS officer and former director of the Intelligence Bureau. Presently he is the national security adviser of India. He was born on January 20, 1945 in the Pauri Garhwal district of Uttarakhand during the pre-independence British era. His father's name is Major Gunanand Doval, who is a Garhwali Brahmin.

Ajit Doval and his wife have two children.

Retired IPS officer Ajit Kumar Doval is the fifth and current national security adviser of India.

Introduction to His Life

Doval's father Major G.N. Doval was an officer in the Indian Army.

Full Name	:	Ajit Kumar Doval
Date of Birth	:	January 20, 1945
Place of Birth	:	Pauri Garhwal, Uttarakhand
Nationality	:	Indian
Religion	:	Hindu
Caste	:	Garhwali Brahmin
Work	:	Former IPS, former IB director, current national security adviser
Father's Name	:	Gunanand Doval
Wife	:	Anu Doval
Sons	:	Vivek Doval and Shaurya Doval

Education

Ajit Doval received his early education from Ajmer Military School in Ajmer, Rajasthan. He earned a postgraduate degree in economics from Agra University in 1967. He was awarded an honorary doctorate degrees from Agra University in December 2017 in science, and in May 2018 from Kumaon University in literature. He was awarded an honorary doctorate in philosophy by Amity University in November 2018.

Career

- Ajit Doval's first posting was in the state of Kerala in 1968 after being selected for the Kerala cadre in IPS. About a year and a half later, communal riots broke out in Thalasseri in the Kannur district, which the then police officers were unable to control. At that time M.Karunakaran was the home minister of Kerala. He decided to send Ajit Doval to Thalasseri. After reaching there, Ajit Doval not only put an end to the riots in just two days but also recovered all the goods looted during those riots and returned them to their rightful owners. Owing to this, his image emerged as a go-to man in crisis.
- During that time, he was actively involved during the militant movement in Punjab and Mizoram. Ajit Doval spent a considerable amount of time inside the Burma and China borders with the Mizo National Front. His performance was memorable even during the rebellion of the Mizo National Front.

He weakened the Mizo National Front and established peace in Mizoram.

- Ajit Doval was one of the three officers who negotiated on behalf of the country on the issue of the release of kidnapped passengers of IC-814 in Kandahar in 1999. He has experience of being an interlocutor during all 15 plane hijacking incidents that took place from 1971–1999.
- Ajit Doval headed the operational wing of the IB for more than a decade. In addition, he was also the founding chairman of the Multi-Agency Centre (MAC) and the Joint Task Force on intelligence.
- Ajit Doval also received training from India's third National Security Adviser M.K. Narayanan for counter-terrorism operations.
- Before 'Operation Black Thunder' took place in the year 1988, he had gathered important information by entering the Golden Temple.
- Ajit Doval spent almost seven years in Pakistan in the guise of a Muslim. During that time, he collected a lot of important information for Indian security agencies.
- He retired from the post of director of the Intelligence Bureau in January 2005. The

year 2014 marked a turning point in his career and he was appointed as the fifth national security adviser of India.

- From 2009–2011, he contributed to the editing of the report titled 'Indian Black Money Abroad in Secret Banks and Tax Heaven' and he became a pivotal part of this campaign of the BJP.
- In 2014, Ajit Doval was instrumental in the release of 46 Indian nurses who were trapped in Iraq and whose families had lost contact with them. For that, he personally went to Iraq and worked on a secret mission.
- Ajit Doval, along with the Chief of Army Staff, also played a key role in the operation against terrorists operating outside Myanmar. The operation proved to be successful, which neutralised 50 terrorists.
- Ajit Doval is also credited with making changes in Indian security policies regarding Pakistan. His role in the 2016 surgical strike is also considered important. It is said that due to his plan, India was successful in achieving its goal.
- In 2018, he was appointed as the chairman of the Strategic Policy Group. Apart from this, Ajit Doval's role has also been seminal in the

retaliatory action by the Indian Air Force in response to the Pulwama terror attack. He has also played a crucial role along with the army chiefs in discharging the responsibility of keeping the Indian Army ready against the action taken by Pakistan.

James Bond of India

After he successfully handled the Kerala communal riots, Ajit Doval was called to Delhi in the year 1972. He was appointed in IB. He was called 'James Bond' at that time. After joining, he was posted in Mizoram. He himself had asked for that posting because, at that time, the rebellion of the 'Mizo National Front' was at its peak. Mizo rebels had declared war on the Indian Army by demanding an independent Mizoram. There was rampant violence. There were constant attacks on the police and the army. Weapons were being supplied from Pakistan.

Ajit Doval went there as a secret agent. He joined the Mizo Front after meeting the rebels. Later, he brainwashed the rebels and then forced them to surrender.

During the Mizo National Front (MNF) insurgency, Doval won over six of Laldenga's seven commanders. He spent several years with the Mizo National Front inside Arakan and the

Chinese territory of Burma. From Mizoram, he went to Sikkim, where he played a vital role during the state's merger with India.

In Sikkim, Ajit Doval played a decisive role. Sikkim also joined India in 1975. He played a key part in the inclusion of Sikkim in India.

Ajit Doval was awarded the 'President's Police Medal' for his outstanding contribution to Mizoram and Sikkim. The speciality of this medal is that this medal is conferred only after completing 14 years of service. But he was awarded it in 1975 only after 7 years of service. It was really a great achievement for him.

Vivekanand International Foundation

In 2019, Ajit Doval became the founding president of the Vivekananda International Foundation.

The foundation is part of the Vivekananda Kendra located in Kanyakumari, which was founded by Eknath Ranade of the Rashtriya Swayamsevak Sangh. Nowadays, Vivekananda Foundation, a think tank based on the ideology of Rashtriya Swayamsevak Sangh, works to provide inputs on relations with neighbouring countries and strategic matters to the Modi government, which includes many retired IAS and IPS officers, scientists and military officers of India. After Ajit

Doval became the national security adviser, N.C. Vij was made the director of the foundation in his place. Apart from former bureaucrats and former army officers associated with the foundation, most people work as volunteers and do not accept a salary.

IC-814 Hijack

This incident took place in 1999. In this incident, Pakistani terrorists hijacked the Indian aircraft IC-814 that flew from Kathmandu. There were 176 Indian passengers on that plane. The terrorists hijacked the plane, taking it first to Lahore and then from Lahore to Kandahar in Afghanistan. All the passengers were taken hostage. Meanwhile, Ajit Doval on behalf of India held talks with the terrorists. The terrorists demanded the handing over of Pakistani terrorists lodged in Indian jails in exchange for the safe release of the passengers. Their demand was met and three terrorists were released; in return, almost all the passengers were returned safely.

Iraq Mission—2014

After a particular incident in 2014, Ajit Doval was appointed the national security adviser of India. In 2014, ISIS terrorists took 46 Indian nurses captive in Iraq. To rescue them, India undertook an intelligence mission, under which Ajit Doval personally went to Iraq to understand the situation on the ground. He interacted with the ISIS terrorists, took them into confidence and successfully brought all the nurses back home safely. Even today at the age of 76, Ajit Doval plays a central role in Indian border security.

Spy in Pakistan

As an undercover operative in Pakistan, Ajit Doval was responsible for gathering information on intelligence and terrorist activities. Big terrorists like Mafia don Dawood Ibrahim were on his target list.

Ajit Doval stayed as a spy of India in Pakistan for seven years. During that time, he lived like a Muslim and did not let anyone know that he was a Hindu. But once a situation arose when his identity was exposed.

He used to live in a Muslim-dominated area of Lahore. There is a very big *Auliya*'s tomb in Lahore, which many people visit. Once, he was passing through that area. At that time, a man called out to him. He had a very long white beard and he looked like a Muslim.

Doval went to him.

The man asked, "Are you a Hindu?"

Doval said, "No, I am a Muslim."

"You're lying! You are a Hindu."

Doval again denied it.

He said, "I know you are a Hindu because your ears are pierced."

In response, Doval said, "I converted to Islam later."

The man said, "No, you haven't converted later either."

Doval asked him how he knew such subtle things. The man said that he was also a Hindu.

He advised Doval to undergo plastic surgery or else his cover might be blown. Later, Doval underwent plastic surgery even though a small hole is still visible in his ear.

Doval is Another Name for Adventure

Doval undertook many such dangerous adventures, which make even the stories of 'James Bond' tame.

Through the surgical strike carried out by the Indian Army across the border in Myanmar, Doval sent a direct and clear message to the enemies of India that now India had adopted an aggressive attitude.

During the important 'Operation Blue Star' carried out by the Indian Army, he played the role of a spy and provided vital intelligence to the Indian security forces, with the help of which the military operation became successful. During the operation, his role was that of a Pakistani spy who had won the trust of Khalistanis and provided information about their preparations.

When Indian Airlines flight IC-814 was hijacked from Kathmandu in 1999, he was appointed India's chief negotiator. Later, that flight was diverted to Kandahar and the passengers were taken hostage.

In Kashmir, too, he did remarkable work and infiltrated militant organisations. He diverted the current of extremism by making the militants, the peacekeepers. He had made Kuka Parray, a prominent anti-India extremist, his biggest informer.

He was also active in the Northeast in the 1980s. At that time, the Mizo National Front under the leadership of Laldenga had spread violence and unrest. But then Doval won the confidence of Laldenga's six out of seven commanders, as a result of which Laldenga was forced to opt for a peace treaty with the Indian Government.

Doval had executed a successful plan to rescue Liviu Radu, a Romanian diplomat who was kidnapped by the Khalistan Liberation Front in 1991.

Doval planned a 'surgical strike' after the attack on the army in Northeast India and the Indian Army took action across the border in Myanmar and killed the militants. The Indian Army carried out the operation in collaboration with the Myanmar Army and the rebels of the NSCN (National Socialist Council of Nagaland) Khaplang faction, in which around 30 militants were killed.

Doval also held diplomatic responsibilities in Pakistan and Britain and then headed the Operations Wing of the Intelligence Bureau for nearly a decade.

First Officer to Receive the 'Kirti Chakra'

Ajit Doval is the only police officer in the country to have been awarded the 'Kirti Chakra'. Usually, this award is only conferred upon army officers; but Ajit Doval has performed many feats, that no one else could have accomplished except him. In 1989, Ajit Doval led 'Operation Black Thunder' to remove extremists from the Golden Temple in

Amritsar. At that time, he worked as a rickshaw wallah and brought out maps, weapons and all the information about the insurgents from the Golden Temple with full secrecy. Similarly, before undertaking the mission as a spy in Pakistan, he also learned to make shoes so that no one would suspect him during intelligence work.

Mastermind of Surgical Strike

The mastermind of the Uri attack, when India carried out a surgical strike on Pakistan was Ajit Doval. The entire operation was carried out under his supervision. India also carried out a surgical strike on Myanmar. That too was executed under his supervision. Under his direction, India has conducted several campaigns to eliminate terrorism from Kashmir.

Doval's Warning

Doval has cautioned in the present context that the method of war has changed. Now countries can also be broken by dividing the society. National Security Adviser Ajit Doval has said that in the changing times, the methods of waging war against any country have also changed. As a new weapon of war, preparations are being made to destroy civil society.

Doval said, "Wars are no longer effective enough to achieve political and military objectives. Actually, wars are very expensive. Not every country can afford them. There is always uncertainty about their outcome. In such a situation, the country can be harmed by dividing the society and spreading confusion."

He said, "People are most important. So, a new front has been opened in the form of the fourth generation of war whose target is society." He said that the length of our border with Pakistan, China, Myanmar and Bangladesh is about 15,000 kilometres and that the police should have a greater role in border management in those areas.

He told the IPS officers, "The responsibility of law and order management of the 32 lakh sq. km area inside India lies with the police force, but now this role will expand further. We have different kinds of problems on our 15,000 kilometres long border. In the future, you will also be responsible for the border management of this country."

An Appraisal of the Main Achievements

- The medal which is given to an IPS Officer after 17 years in service was conferred upon him only after 6 years of service.

- He spent seven years as a spy in Pakistan and during that time, he reached the post of marshal in Amb there.
- He reactivated RAW in Balochistan and made it an international issue.
- He has experience in leading the Operations Wing of IB for more than a decade.
- He received training from India's third National Security Adviser M.K. Narayanan for counter-terrorism operations.
- He spent a long time inside the border of Burma and China with the Mizo National Front.
- In 2018, he was appointed as the chairman of the Strategic Policy Group (SPG).
- He played a key role in the 'rescue operation' of the Romanians in the state of Punjab. Before 'Operation Black Thunder' in 1988, he had gathered important information by entering the Golden Temple.

National Security Adviser Post-Retirement

- Even after retiring from the post of director of the Intelligence Bureau in 2005, he remained active in matters related to India's security. Apart from writing for some famous newspapers and journals, he also gave speeches at government and non-government organisations on issues related to India's security.

- Ajit Doval has held this post since May 30, 2014. He is the fifth national security adviser of India. Earlier, Shivshankar Menon was the national security adviser of India.
- Doval played an important role in the release of 46 Indian nurses who were trapped in Iraq in the year 2014. For that, he personally went to Iraq and worked on a secret mission.
- He also played a pivotal role in the campaign against terrorists inside Myanmar's border, in which 50 terrorists were killed.
- Ajit Doval has worked in the intelligence department for most of his career. According to information received from secret sources, he lived as an intelligence spy in Pakistan for seven years.
- Ajit Doval made a major change in the Indian security policies, as a result of which the response to the Uri terror attack in 2016 was given in the form of 'Surgical Strike'.

Awards and Honours

- Ajit Doval is the youngest officer to receive the Police Medal for his distinguished services.
- He was awarded the 'President's Police Medal'. This medal is presented every year on Republic Day and Independence Day by the president to a selected officer for his gallantry or distinguished service.
- In 1988, Ajit Doval was awarded the 'Kirti Chakra' which is the second-highest gallantry award.
- Ajit Doval is among those people who work 12 months a year, 7 days a week and 24 hours a day for our security even without being on the border.

❑

2
Four-Point Mantra for Success

Prime Minister Modi chose Doval as his national security adviser. It is a position that is more influential than the ministers of Defence and Foreign Affairs. This puts Doval in charge of talks with arch-rival Pakistan.

He visits arms-producing countries to discuss strategic capabilities and plans responses to terrorist attacks by maintaining daily contact with Foreign Secretary S. Jaishankar (now External Affairs Minister), the country's top diplomat.

Doval's influential relations with Modi have given politicians from the opposition parties space for criticism and fuelled discontent within Modi's administration.

After retiring from the Intelligence Bureau, Doval founded the Vivekananda International Foundation in 2009. In 1972, he had moved to the Intelligence Bureau, where he spent three decades, including stints in the troubled areas of the Northeast, Jammu and Kashmir and Uttarakhand.

Ajit Doval said during a lecture, "India has a mindset whereby when it hits, it uses less power than its weight. We have to increase our weight and punch in the same proportion."

Four-Point Mantra of Success

In a world where power dynamics keep changing, only those people will be successful who can understand the changes that are taking place now, have a positive attitude, are attuned to the world around them and are always willing to learn from every person, situation and action. National Security Adviser (NSA) Ajit Doval believes in this.

Doval shared his four-point mantra for success in his acceptance speech after he was conferred an honorary doctorate by Governor K.K. Paul during the 14th convocation ceremony of Kumaon University.

Emphasising that the world and its power dynamics are changing, Doval said, "First the reins of power were in the hands of those who were physically strong, then those who owned large tracts of land, then those who had large armies. Presently, it is in the hands of those who have the technology."

He said that those who were not able to identify the changes taking place around them were unsuccessful. He said, "Only those who can see the changes and who look at the world with a positive attitude, who think that there is much to learn and who see the positivity in every person and every action, will be successful. The doors will be closed for those who have a negative attitude."

Addressing the students, Doval said that 51 years ago he had attended a convocation as a student after completing his postgraduation. "I hope that with the knowledge you have gained here, you will effectively fulfil your responsibilities in the times to come.

"But I have a question. Whatever you have learned here, is it enough for the next 50 years? What kind of a world would it be? What kind of a society would it be? Are you ready for that new world?" he asked.

Sharing a story, Doval said that when the Buddha was on his deathbed, his disciple Ananda asked him who would show him the way after he left the physical body. The Buddha gave him a mantra, '*Appa Deepo Bhava*', or be the light unto yourself. You can learn everywhere in this world. If your mind is in harmony, it will receive knowledge from all sides. He said, "Be your own guru and disciple."

On receiving the honorary degree, Doval said, "I was told about this honour a year ago; but I was somewhat reluctant. I am not from academia. I have been an 'operation man' all my life. I accept this honour with humility and gratitude."

University Chancellor K.K. Paul said, "Today is a very special day indeed. Kumaon University has honoured itself in a way by honouring our most esteemed son, Ajit Doval."

In his address, the chief minister said that a professor who taught in America had once told him that Uttarakhand has many human resources but lacks professionalism. He urged the youth to develop entrepreneurship, skills and professionalism and contribute to the development of the state and stop migration outside the state.

❑

3

India's 'Human Capital'

Noting that China has a large reserve of rare earth in the world while India has less, National Security Adviser Ajit Doval said that the country can counter this by converting its demographic dividend, i. e. 'young population' into an asset. Speaking at an event, he said that India envisages becoming a major power and needs to use its 'scarce human wealth' (130 crore population with 50 per cent population below 25 years of age) as other major powers including China.

Addressing the students at the convocation ceremony of Amity University, Noida, Doval said, "These days, what is happening in the world is that there is a transformation in technology, weapons, industry and trade and we find the one thing that's going to make the biggest difference is what you call 'rare earth', which includes radioactive material, uranium and other high-potential materials."

He said, "Rare earth is an important, non-renewable natural resource, and alloys are used in many tools of everyday use, such as computer memory, rechargeable batteries, cell phones, catalytic converters, magnets, fluorescent lighting, etc.

"How will India, which envisions to be a major power in the world, compete in a world where assets such as natural resources cannot compete with the powers with which we wish to compete and not necessarily in a conflicting manner? We have found one resource and that is the 'rare human wealth' of 130 crore people and 50 per cent of which is below 25 years of age.

"Just imagine if this 'rare earth' could be transformed into those high-technology things, the value of 'human wealth' would be unimaginable!"

He said that a huge, young manpower cannot be an asset in itself unless it is channelised properly.

He observed that in the thousands of years of history of this country, we have the youngest generation, which has vast opportunities.

Calling upon the youth to develop knowledge and skills, he affirmed, "If the youth is not channelised by employing them profitably, then it can be a source of big problems. If one has the right capabilities and intentions, then they can be channelised and this is the right perspective to serve the country."

He advised the students that the overall progress of life can be guided and evaluated by keeping in mind three important points—correct assessment of the knowledge as to where you currently stand, focus on where you want to be and the path to follow.

Doval said, "The problem with Indian youth is that they spend too much time dreaming about where they should be in the future, which is important; but it is also necessary to pay attention to the path."

❑

4

Peace Ambassador Ajit Doval

From the 1972 Kerala riots to the recent Jammu and Kashmir unrest, Doval has been at the forefront of the crisis.

National Security Adviser Ajit Doval was recently seen walking through the violence-hit suburbs of Northeast Delhi as a 'peace ambassador' on behalf of the BJP government. Prime Minister Narendra Modi and Home Minister Amit Shah had directly entrusted Doval with the task of ensuring the restoration of peace in Delhi.

Doval met the victims soon after US President Donald Trump left Delhi after his visit. He made a late-night visit to the violence-hit areas. He again visited the affected areas along with senior officials, where he met the local people and assured them that the situation was under control.

Doval, the 'Indian James Bond', had done something similar in Kerala long back in 1972. This 1968 batch Kerala cadre IPS officer was instrumental in overpowering the infamous Thalasseri riots, the tenth major communal riot the country had witnessed and the first for Kerala.

Clashes broke out between the two communities during the last days of 1971 and by the first week of 1972, the tension had taken the form of full-fledged Hindu-Muslim riots. It started on December 28 when a shoe was thrown at a religious procession. The RSS was accused of targeting Muslims and their mosques. The CPI(M) sided with the Muslims and the clashes escalated. Realising that the situation was getting out of hand, the then Home Minister K Karunakaran apparently sought out the 'smartest policemen' to entrust the task of ending the violence and found one of the junior IPS officers at the time—Ajit Doval posted as ASP in Kottayam.

Doval, who reached Thalasseri, the epicentre of the violence, visited all the affected areas soon after taking charge. He asked the victims to return to their homes and promised to round up all the robbers before the law. He also assured the victims that all their looted items would be brought back.

Doval, who was then in his third year of service, proved his point. The riot was controlled within a week of his arrival.

Doval was in charge of law and order in Kannur for four months before joining the IB. The rest of his life is certainly an interesting chapter in the history of Indian espionage.

According to a 2007 Home Ministry report, which studied major riots in the country, the first phase of unrest in the Thalasseri riots was pre-planned by anti-social elements. The second phase was in the nature of retaliation by the Muslims and the third phase was retaliation by the Hindus.

There may or may not be similarities between the two unrests, but Doval must have known what he had to do as he walked through those narrow streets.

❑

5
Superspy Doval

Before him, no spy had been capable of carrying out a carefully designed counter-terrorism operation deep inside enemy territory. He has personally trained agents in the dangerous art of conducting a full search of insurgent hideouts in troubled Kashmir, posing a great risk to life and liberty. For decades, he has worked to track down suspected terrorists in dangerous areas of the Northeast, infiltrate terrorist organisations in Punjab and conduct dangerous counter-terrorism operations, and most importantly, he has acted as a father figure to the spies of India who work thousands of miles away. No other Indian agent had dared to make an attempt in the past away from home, away from covert operations, perhaps with the exception of General Vikram Singh dismantling the Technical Services Division.

Ajit Kumar Doval, the former director of the Intelligence Bureau and now the new national security adviser in the Modi government is a respected figure in the secret world of Indian espionage. As a field agent, the 'Master' had successfully broken the back of the Northeast insurgency in 1986 in an undercover operation that brought him lasting fame—the defection of six out of seven commanders of Laldenga's organisation for India's cause and forcing the separatists to sign a peace deal.

Doval's addiction to danger during his heydays as an operative, drafting and signing INT reports instead of staying safely behind a government officer's desk in the North Block marks his greatness. As a young man, he sought an exciting life. Veteran intelligence analysts believe that the 'Doval effect' also affects the PMO's aggressive foreign policy towards Pakistan and China.

Hours after the formal announcement of his appointment, discussions between terrorists on the Kashmir border revealed that terrorist commanders in Pakistan-occupied Kashmir (PoK) were on the knife-edge. India's most wanted Dawood Ibrahim, who was a prized guest of ISI in Karachi, immediately shifted his base near the Pak-Afghan border.

D.C. Pathak, former director of the Intelligence Bureau who worked with Doval, noted that the appointment of the NSA by the government was completely in line with the task. "The challenges and problems we face are well known to everybody. Now we have the right man for the job. I have always advocated that someone with a field operations background should be an NSA."

In 1988, Jarnail Singh Bhindranwale of Amritsar dominated the area around the Golden Temple. Khalistani militants noticed a rickshaw puller in the area. Though he seemed quite ordinary, he was new in that area. The suspected terrorists put him on their watch list. The rickshaw puller assured the militants that he was an ISI worker sent by his Pakistani masters to help with Khalistan. Two days before 'Operation Black Thunder', the rickshaw puller entered the Golden Temple and returned with vital information including the actual strength and position of the terrorists inside the shrine. He was none other than undercover agent Ajit Doval. The young police officer was inside Harmandir Sahib when the last attack took place, giving the security forces the information they needed to conduct a search and flush operation.

An intelligence officer who met Doval after 'Operation Black Thunder' says, "His piercing gaze and mysterious smile are etched in my memory forever. The risk was high, but our security forces received the blueprint for the attack from Doval. Details like maps, strength, weapons and hideouts of terrorists were given by him. IB gave information to NSG in order to save countless lives and prevent further damage to the Golden Temple."

Similarly, his campaigns in Mizoram in the 1980s achieved unprecedented success in eliminating and influencing the surrender of important rebel leaders. Doval's strategy was to use information from agents on the ground to crack down on the rebels, while undercover operations were carried out against the hard-line traitors. An intelligence officer working under Doval describes his casual style towards trusted agents engaged in field operations— "They were encouraged to 'live' their roles and without being questioned; they could come to work wearing whatever they liked."

The officer recalled, "We didn't need to dress like *babus*. The operatives could come dressed in *kurtas, pyjamas, lungis* and wearing sandals. Anyone who was preparing for a session in enemy territory was allowed to grow a beard 'to get into the role'. Others could hire clerics to learn Urdu and Arabic. As part of their cover, some agents spent days learning to make shoes and later worked as cobblers in targeted areas, including overseas areas." The officers say proudly, "Doval Sahib himself is an expert in Urdu."

The surrender of the dreaded Kashmiri terrorist Kuka Parray in the 90s was a remarkable feat for Doval. Such was his skill that armed with a terrorist psychological profile, he was able to brainwash and persuade Kuka Parray and his gang to become rebels. A serving intelligence operative who had witnessed the action in Kashmir as a young man admitted, "He met Parray at some point in the 1990s and inspired him to help the government," and declined to give more details. Kuka Parray and his organisation 'Ikhwan-e-Muslimoon' with the help of the Indian Army killed top terrorist commanders in the valley. Kuka Parray was also a political victory. The operation later enabled the centre to hold assembly elections in Jammu and Kashmir in 1996. Kuka Parray, who became an MLA after the elections, was later killed in a terrorist attack.

The official says that at that time New Delhi was not sure that Doval would succeed. He was aware of the complex political situation, but the coup also earned him the respect of his staunch critics within the agency, who advocated a peace policy with Pakistan-sponsored terror outfits. The maestro of psychological warfare, Doval's role in many fairy-tale adventures in Kashmir ranged from just a ruthless spy to a shrewd strategist who brought various separatists to the negotiating table, including Yasin Malik, Shabir Shah, Maulvi Farooq, and even the pro-Pak SAS.

Intelligence agents admit that although 'India's George Smiley' had resigned from his position in 2005, he was still informally directing covert missions in the region. In August 2005, a WikiLeaks cable reported that Doval had planned an IB operation to apprehend Dawood. But Dawood fled after some insider informers in the Mumbai Police apprised him. "The reports of Dawood changing his base in Pakistan seem credible as Doval has been following him for over a decade," said an intelligence official.

Doval's New Strategy

- To strengthen, revive and ensure coordination between the security and intelligence systems that has been systematically destroyed by the regime.

- Maximising the authority of security agencies undermined by the bureaucratic system to deal with cross-border terrorism.
- To formulate a strong policy to deal with Pakistan and other neighbouring countries that are known for giving shelter.
- To strengthen and ensure the penetration of human intelligence at the district and local levels.
- Creating a National Intelligence Grid for integration of intelligence.
- Developing an anti-Naxal policy.
- Ensuring that the innocents are fully protected and the cases of those in jail are resolved expeditiously.

❑

6
Surgical Strike and Ajit Doval

An elite group of the Indian Army conducted surgical strikes across the Line of Control, in which 35–40 terrorists were killed in Pakistan-occupied Kashmir. The pre-planned surgical strike by para-commandos marked a change in the Indian policy of 'strategic restraint'. But for the first time on October 7, 2014, National Security Adviser Ajit Doval ordered the armed forces to respond with 'full force' to Pakistan at the slightest provocation. After the surgical strike, there was celebration among the people of India. Some gave credit to Narendra Modi and the Indian Army, but very few people know that Ajit Doval was behind the strike.

As part of the new standard operating procedures, Ajit Doval spent Thursday night in the War Room in South Block, which houses the Defence Ministry. The entire operation was closely monitored by Ajit Doval, Defence Minister Manohar Parrikar and Chief of Army Staff General Dalbir Singh. It is believed that India first took an aggressive stance after the BJP came to power in 2014, and especially after Ajit Doval was appointed as India's fifth national security adviser.

What Happened Inside the War Room?

According to a report, at around 11 pm on Wednesday night, the three—Ajit Doval, Manohar Parrikar and General Dalbir Singh reached the war room separately and stayed there till the operation was over. The para-commandos reached their base safely. A close source described the atmosphere in the war room and compared it to the night when Osama bin Laden was killed by US special forces and US security officials, including

President Barack Obama, closely monitored the situation.

The Indian Army first targeted terrorist locations within 20 kilometres of Pakistan-occupied Kashmir and fired heavy artillery. The terrorists were then tracked down by drones till they took shelter at their launch pads near the Line of Control. About a dozen terrorists had taken shelter at each of the launching pads. The para-commandos, who were paradropped on the spot, surrounded the launching pads and killed around 35-40 terrorists.

There were also rumours that the casualties of terrorists could be much higher as official figures are not shared by both India and Pakistan. A close source inside the war room said that while some terrorists scrambled for security, some were hacked and others sought shelter at the launch pads along the Line of Control. Some believe that around 60 people were killed in this operation and at least 10 Pakistani army personnel were killed. But it seems the actual number of casualties may never be known.

It is quite surprising that before the 'Surgical Strike' there was no standard operating procedure for such operations in India. After the Kandahar plane hijacking, the then NSA Brajesh Mishra and Ajit Doval's boss had put in place such procedures four times, which were later removed by the government.

❑

7

Secret Mission in Iraq

India's consular access to repatriate Indians held hostage by insurgents in Iraq was conducted by National Security Adviser Ajit Doval and Intelligence Bureau director Asif Ibrahim. India's consular outreach to bring home 46 nurses, as well as help thousands of other Indians in Iraq to leave the violence-hit country, was conducted by Ajit Doval and Asif Ibrahim, who flew to Baghdad and Riyadh respectively.

In their mission, which was kept secret at the time, information was being shared via phone calls by External Affairs Minister Sushma Swaraj with her counterparts in the region.

At the end of June 2014, the situation seemed complicated for 46 nurses in Tikrit as well as 39 men in Mosul. There was no real intelligence available about the rebel groups. The ISI had captured several cities, including Tikrit, Mosul and the Baiji refinery. In many places they were aided by Ba'athist groups and rebel military commanders who were still loyal to the residual regime of Saddam Hussein, making the task more difficult.

Faced with a dire situation, Prime Minister Narendra Modi asked Doval to convene a high-level meeting to discuss the latest intelligence on the fighting in Tikrit and Mosul as well as the possibilities of evacuating all Indians in Iraq. A day after the meeting, on June 25, 2014, Doval went to Iraq on a top-secret mission to understand the situation on the ground and make high-level contacts in the Iraqi Government.

Since the conflict zone in Iraq was mainly managed by Sunni insurgents and terrorist groups, Ibrahim was sent to Riyadh on June 25–26 to talk to senior officials about intelligence on these groups.

Deep black smoke rose from the emergency ward of their hospital when four terrorists forced M.J. Nityamol and 45 other Indian nurses to board a bus. The walls of the hospital were splashed with blood due to the blast.

At that time, 29-year-old Nityamol in the desert of Saddam Hussein's home town of Tikrit in Iraq, trembled with fear of death. She and her companions had been ordered by the Islamic State of Iraq and Syria (ISIS) fighters to come out of the hospital a few moments ago.

Assault rifles hung from the shoulders of those fighters. They wore dark glasses and their faces were covered with black cloths. As Nityamol looked on, one of the fighters suddenly turned around. He aimed his assault rifle towards the upper floor of the Tikrit Teaching Hospital and started firing randomly.

On that floor was the nurses' residence and workplace. For a week, all the nurses had taken shelter there, avoiding bullets and bomb blasts. As soon as the fighter opened fire, all the windows of the floor shattered and glass pieces rained on the nurses. The terrified nurses started screaming. Some of them ran towards their three injured companions, who were covered in blood due to the raining glass pieces.

The bus moved on. During the eight-hour journey to Mosul, the nurses cried, hugged and comforted each other, praying. The bus passed through winding roads. Maybe the roads weren't safe. The nurses had no idea where they were being taken. There were thick curtains on the windows of the bus.

At the front of the bus was a black flag and a banner, which had something written in Arabic, perhaps to alert the militant companions on the way not to fire at them. A van carrying the belongings of the nurses came behind the bus. Three militants travelled in a dusty old car and the fourth was in the bus with the nurses.

All those 46 nurses had reached Iraq only a few months ago. An agency in Delhi had taken ₹ 1.5 lakhs from each of them in return for a job and had promised them a salary of 750 dollars per month. Twenty-five-year-old Nina Joseph, one of the nurses who is now trying to forget the painful incident at her home in Talayolaparambu in Kottayam, says, "We accepted the job offer because several nurses, whom we know, were already working in Iraq. Those nurses told us that they had had no problem there."

The first team of 33 nurses had reached Iraq on August 16 the previous year. The remaining 13 nurses had arrived there in February this year. Upon reaching the hospital in Tikrit, the nurses were confined to the hospital building. Nityamol said, "We were not allowed to go out. Our connection to the city was only through the sky visible from the window of the second floor, where all the nurses were accommodated, with 6 in a room."

They were first exposed to this new reality in Iraq on June 12, 2014, when gunshots were heard around the hospital and the night was illuminated by a burning building. Soon after, Iraqi nurses whispered to them that they were leaving the city. The Indian nurses had understood that they were now trapped.

However, there was still one recourse left. Their cell phones still worked and they had the Indian Embassy's numbers.

Nityamol said, "On June 13, we called Ajay Kumar, the Indian ambassador to Baghdad, and requested him to evacuate us." All except one of the 46 nurses were from Kerala. So, they called the chief minister of Kerala, Oommen Chandy. Sandra Sebastian, 25, a nurse from Ramapuram in Kottayam, said, "He consoled us and promised help. He also said that the roads in Tikrit had been closed, so it was not safe to travel in such conditions."

The wards of that huge hospital in Tikrit were emptying. Nurses spent their time watching the news on television and on internet on their mobiles. However, after some time, there was no reception on television and the internet did not work. Now they had no idea what was going on in the outside world.

Nityamol said, "For some time, we assumed that there was a fight going on in Tikrit between two local factions. But soon the panes of our windows began to tremble due to the explosions outside. The blasts also occurred repeatedly." One day, they received a call from the Department of Immigrant Keralites Affairs, government of Kerala; information including their passport numbers was also taken to shift them from there.

After a few days, the hospital ran out of food items. If a merciful Iraqi officer had not shown courage, those nurses would have starved. The officer had arranged enough food for all the nurses for the next two weeks. Nityamol says, "We only knew him by the name of Dr. Mohammad of Iraq's health department. He lived near the hospital and whenever we gave a missed call on his mobile, he would immediately come to our aid."

At the end of June, Dr. Mohammad told the nurses that he would no longer be there to help them. He said the insurgents were marching forward and would capture the hospital in no time. By that time, the two Iraqi soldiers guarding the hospital had disappeared.

The next day, the insurgents reached the hospital. Nityamol said, "They wore black clothes, black scarves and sunglasses. We were very scared. They had also brought some severely injured comrades with them and they asked us to dress their wounds and treat them."

On the morning of June 30, the insurgents asked them to vacate the hospital by 6:45 pm. The nurses then called Oman Chandy and Ajay Kumar. Nityamol recounted, "Both of them told us to obey the fighters, as not listening to them could be fatal. But they did not return that evening."

On July 2, the hospital was shaken by a bomb blast. Emergency wards and blood banks collapsed. There were explosions all around. Nityamol saw a building engulfed in flames at a distance of 100 metres. She said, "Cars and trucks were scattered on the streets. There was a smell of burning flesh from the emergency ward."

Nityamol said, "The insurgents arrived that evening and asked us to pack our bags in five hours and go with them." Then the nurses called the Indian Embassy and Chandy. "Both of them told us to remain calm and that the Indian

Government was doing everything possible to save us." But that day also no insurgent returned to pick them up.

But the very next day they arrived. Sebastian said, "They came around 11:30 am and asked us to come out of the hospital within 15 minutes. They told us that they were going to bomb the hospital but that they would take us with them to Mosul. We immediately called up the Indian Embassy. The embassy official said that we should request the insurgents to set us free, but if they did not agree, then we should go with them. He said that if the situation worsened, the government could also try the option of a commando operation to save us." Soon after, the weeping nurses boarded the bus parked outside the hospital.

The insurgents reassured the nurses that they would not be harmed. They also said that they would be taken to Mosul, from where they would be set free at Erbil airport. As the bus started moving, the mobile phones of some nurses started ringing. The nurses did not know who was calling them from New Delhi. The callers asked them to peep through the window to see the place's name on the signboard and to message the name of the place.

In Mosul, they were asked to get off the bus in groups of ten. Nityamol said, "We thought that they wanted to kill us and that was why they asked us to queue up. We were terribly scared. Eventually, we were taken through a corridor to a hall, which had four ACs which looked brand new from their packaging.

"We were still afraid that the fighters would use us to extort a substantial amount of money from the Indian Government. The man guarding us asked us to cover our heads, arms and legs." He gave the nurses *roti*, *dal* and cheese to eat. After that, he brought some mats and asked the nurses to rest.

Throughout the journey, the Indian Embassy had kept in touch with the nurses through messages on mobiles. Their prepaid mobiles were also recharged. Unfortunately, there was no power switch in the room in which the nurses were staying, so one by one the batteries of their phones ran out.

On July 4, 2014, the nurses were told to get ready to go to the airport. The nurses called the Indian Ambassador Ajay Kumar. He asked the nurses to go along with the insurgents. Their bus was stopped three times on the way to the airport; probably by other insurgents. Nityamol said, "We were asked to get down at one place and go inside a building. Thankfully, the house had a power switch where we could charge our phones.

But there was no mobile signal. Two of the nurses had SIMs from another company and we spoke to the ambassador through them. He told us that a car was parked outside the building and the name of the driver was Abdul Shah. We should sit in it after asking the driver his name. But upon coming out, we did not see any vehicle, nor was there any driver."

Nityamol said, "Later, some of the insurgents returned and asked us to board a bus. The bus took us to a place where some Indian Embassy officials were waiting for us. Those officers took us to Erbil International Airport at 8:45 pm." However, this suggests that the Indian Embassy was in contact with the insurgents at least during the last round of the nurses' journey. But the Indian Government has been silent on this. Eventually, the nurses boarded the plane at 4:10 am on July 5.

Ajit Doval was instrumental in the release of 46 Indian nurses who were trapped in Iraq and whose families had also lost contact with them. He had personally gone to Iraq and worked on a secret mission.

❑

8
Cross-Border Operation in Myanmar

In the worst attack in two decades, 18 soldiers of the Indian Army were killed in an ambush by militants on a convoy of the 6 Dogra Regiment in Manipur on June 4. What happened next could very well be the script of a hair-raising thriller.

The army retaliated, killing at least 15 insurgents responsible for the attack on its troops. The army's Special Forces conducted a surgical strike outside Indian territory and inside Myanmar striking two terrorist groups believed to be NSCN(K) and KYKL.

National Security Adviser Ajit Doval, former director of Intelligence Bureau and an expert in counter-insurgency operations, accompanied Prime Minister Narendra Modi on his visit to Bangladesh. He was not to be found with Prime Minister Modi during the visit as he was in Manipur and was supervising the coordination of intelligence agencies.

The result—the army, air force and other major agencies coordinated one of the rarest operations to raid terrorists across the border in Myanmar.

But how did Myanmar, a sovereign nation, allow Indian security forces to conduct operations on its land?

A few days ago, the then Foreign Secretary S. Jaishankar had made a quiet visit to Myanmar, the details of which were not given. His visit was probably in line with the long military cooperation between the two countries and the Myanmar Government's silence on Tuesday's operation was proof that Jaishankar's visit was a huge success.

Both countries have been working together against the insurgents of the Northeast for a long time. In 2001, the Myanmar Army reportedly helped in the elimination of some terrorist hideouts in Manipur. In April–May 1995, 'Operation Golden Bird' was launched as an Indo-Myanmar joint operation, in which about 40 terrorists were killed.

Reports suggested that New Delhi received consent from the Myanmar Government on Monday for a plan to fly in special forces to attack three insurgent camps, 15–20 kilometres across the border, in the dense forests of Myanmar's Western Sagaing Division. Colonel Gaurav Sharma, Defence Attaché at the Indian Embassy, shared the details of the operation with the Myanmar Army after Ambassador Gautam Mukhopadhyay received a high-level clearance.

The operation was a testament to the collaboration between various agencies and ministries of the government. Meanwhile, the attack on the army has again raised the question as to whether the responsibility of guarding the Indo-Myanmar border should be given to the BSF instead of the Assam Rifles. The border guarding capability of the Assam Rifles has long been questioned as it operates from positions located far away from the border.

NSA Ajit Doval recently said that the decision to deploy BSF to guard the border was taken last year, but now it is being reviewed in the light of the

'Look East' policy. In 2010, the Ministry of Home Affairs initiated discussions with the Defence Ministry about delegating the responsibility to the BSF (which reports to the Home Ministry) besides fencing the border, but it hasn't come into effect yet.

In light of the latest intelligence inputs, the NSCN(K) is operating virtually out of Myanmar bases near the border and has tacit support from China. This move is now getting immense encouragement. Most of the cadre of NSCN(K) are Nagas belonging to Myanmar. A former PLA soldier runs an arms factory near the border, while some Chinese officials are reported to be in constant touch with Khaplang (who heads the NSCN).

Union Minister Rajyavardhan Singh Rathore had lauded the army's operation saying the prime minister had led the Indian Army to 'chase' militants in Myanmar, in which two terror camps were completely destroyed.

These extremists have become used to attacking the Indian Army or paramilitary forces or civilians in the country and then fleeing to safe havens. They are convinced that the Indian armed forces will not pursue them. However, our prime minister has taken a very bold step. The message is now very clear to all those who harboured the intention of terror in our country.

Although the fuming Modi government wanted a covert raid across the border in Myanmar within 24 hours of the dastardly attack on the Indian Army on 4, June, Army Chief General Dalbir Singh Suhag said that the time for operational preparedness was too short and he gave precise advice that the strike should be carried out within 72 hours.

In a meeting on the evening of June 4, two options were discussed intensively—all around aerial bombardment of the camps using Sukhoi and MIG-29s or a ground attack by 21 Para commandos. At the meeting chaired by Home Minister Rajnath Singh, National Security Adviser Ajit Doval, Defence Minister Manohar Parrikar, Army Chief and IB and RAW chiefs, finally the decision of on-ground operations by special forces was taken as airstrikes could have caused 'collateral damage' to civilians. Also, women or children were present in the camps. "Any collateral damage could have led to international condemnation," a top government official said.

On the basis of ground reports received from Manipur and Nagaland, the Home Ministry officials put the casualties of the insurgents at 38 while the army gave the death toll of around 20. "We expected more damage, but it seems that the rebels sensed the impending action and fled. The operation, which started at 3 am on June 9, was monitored live by top government officials from Delhi."

At the June 4 meeting, it was the idea of Rajnath Singh and Manohar Parrikar to launch a strike early in the morning of June 5 as pinpointed intelligence about the presence of insurgent camps in Myanmar was available and initial inputs suggested that the attackers had gone back to those camps. However, General Suhag said that 72 hours were needed to prepare a precise attack design. Government sources said that on June 5, General Suhag and Ajit Doval went to Manipur to assess the 'strike-capability' and the plan was to launch the strike on the morning of June 8. But after the prime minister went to Bangladesh on July 6–7, the security establishment decided to wait for Modi's return and delayed the operation by a day so that the plan could be explained personally in detail to the prime minister. Modi returned on the night of June 7 and Doval and General Suhag briefed him about the plan on the morning of June 8. The prime minister immediately gave the green signal.

On the night of June 8, the Army Aviation Wing in its advanced light helicopters dropped the commandos at a distance from the rebel camps so that they would not be alerted by the sound of helicopters. After that, the soldiers entered on foot for the final attack. In addition to killing the rebels, terrorist infrastructure in the camps was also destroyed by the raiding commandos.

❑

9

The 'Double Squeeze' Strategy

Pakistan, today, said National Security Adviser Ajit Doval's strategy of 'aggressive defence and double pressure' to make India a regional hegemony will never succeed.

Exercising its right to respond at the UN General Assembly, Pakistan said that it was 'unfortunate that India had chosen to criticise Prime Minister Shahid Khaqan Abbasi's statement on Kashmir, which reflected the feelings and aspirations of the oppressed and subjugated'.

Tipu Usman, counsellor of Pakistan's Permanent Mission to the United Nations, said, "The aggressive defence and double squeeze strategy by NSA Doval, which India believes can make it a territorial hegemony, will never succeed."

Pakistan said, "Indian operatives of devastation and terrorism like Commander Jadhav were caught red-handed while causing sabotage in Pakistan. Terrorism and spies can never fulfil Indian dreams, which will remain only dreams."

The diplomat said the 'pain' of the Kashmiri people at the hands of Indian security forces is being documented by the international community and rights organisations.

He said that the people of Kashmir look to the members of the international community, especially the UN Security Council, to fulfil their pledge to hold a free and fair plebiscite under the backing of the United Nations so that they can decide their future.

He said, "I want to re-emphasise and refute all the misconceptions that India wants to build. India is responsible for undermining regional peace and stability."

A Pakistani diplomat alleged that at least 10 civilians, including several women, had lost their lives from the Pakistani side due to unprovoked firing and mortar shelling by Indian forces along the Line of Control in Jammu and Kashmir. The Pakistani diplomat said, "The shelling continues unabated, which is a sad reminder of Indian stubbornness and obstinacy. This too will fail."

India, exercising its right to respond after Pakistan Prime Minister Shahid Khaqan Abbasi raised the Kashmir issue at the UN General Assembly, called Pakistan a 'terrorist' and said it 'has become synonymous with terror'—a prosperous 'industry' producer and exporters of global terrorism.

Abbasi accused India of indulging in terror activities against his country and warned of a 'corresponding reaction' if it 'carries out activities across the LoC' or works on 'principles of limited war against Pakistan'. He urged the United Nations to appoint a special envoy to Kashmir as he claimed that the struggle of the people of the region was being 'brutally suppressed' by India.

❑

10

The 'Doval Doctrine' and Diverting India's Stand on Beijing

Doval's remarks assume particular significance amid reports that China is gradually increasing its naval presence in the Indian Ocean.

Doval, who was referred to as 'The Hawkish Doval' by former RAW chief A S Dulat, is known for his hard-line stance in negotiations on border disputes with China.

His rare public interactions since taking over as the NSA have shown that Doval prefers to rely on military solutions rather than negotiations. When India's traditional policy in dealing with border disputes with its neighbours promoted a defensive approach, it was Doval who pioneered the concept of a defensive-offensive and aggressive foreign policy.

When asked about his views on talks with China, it was the current NSA who remarked that 'India will not compromise on its territorial interests and sovereignty.'

An article in the *Asia Times* in 2016 commented on Doval's statement: "He (Doval) said at the Munich Security Conference in New Delhi in October 2014 that 'India will not compromise on its regional interests', whereas its original purpose was to reach a settlement on the dispute in the meeting of the special representatives of both the countries."

The influence of Doval's policy ideas, which apparently pervaded the foreign policy of the Modi government, is so different from that of his predecessors that his views on the territorial disputes of China, Pakistan and India are now commonly known as the 'Doval Doctrine'.

Responding to a question on how to deal with China's growing power, Doval admitted that China's military is much stronger than India even as the former Intelligence Bureau director lauded India's missile technology. He said that it was difficult for India to counter China's might in the next 50 years; but he advocated developing missile technology to target China's economic installations, which he said was the Dragon's only weak spot.

Doval's earlier comments on China's 'relentless regional hunger' are significant. The NSA's earlier comments assume significance as China is gradually increasing its naval presence in the Indian Ocean and has conducted military exercises in Tibet even as the border standoff in Sikkim continues.

A report cited Doval's remarks at the 2014 Munich Security Conference. Doval had said that even though relations with China are very important, India should not compromise on the issues of sovereignty. Doval said, "I want to develop our relations to such an extent, till our territorial and integral sovereignty ... we won't be able to compromise on it."

Doval's remarks assume significance at a time when China is ramping up anti-India rhetoric in what it sees as an unprecedented dispute with New Delhi. India and China have been locked in a standoff for more than three weeks after the Chinese military attempted to build a road on the disputed narrow land in the Doklam area in the Sikkim sector near the Bhutan trijunction. China made it clear that the result of back-channel talks will be fruitful only after India withdrew its forces.

While Narendra Modi, under Doval's influence, has been adamant in urging China to 'reconsider' its position on the current disputes with India, Doval's predecessor Brajesh Mishra had seen considerable progress in Sino-India relations and was hoping to reach positive results.

❑

11

India's Aggressive Stand on the Border

Indian Army's message to Pakistan through 'Surgical Strike' was clear and simple—if you mess with us, we will hit you back. The attack is seen as a major change in India's policy of restraint with Pakistan. This essentially means that the country can strike back at will, including retrospectively, to combat cross-border terror.

This aggressive stance is the brainchild of none other than National Security Adviser Ajit

Doval. On October 7, 2014, Doval summoned the director general and general of BSF and asked them to 'fire at will' with 'full force' at the slightest provocation through cross-border firing by Pakistan.

Doval said, "You answer with two for one bullet fired by them." The idea was to systematically destroy their infrastructure until the ceasefire violations from the other side ceased.

Ever since Doval has taken office, he has supported the nationalist agenda by taking a tough stand against hostile neighbours. India's policy changes in the last two years have boosted the morale of the security forces while Islamabad has got a clear message that if the proxy war against India continues, 'it will shed more blood'. Sameer Patil, who served in the prime minister's National Security Council Secretariat under the previous Congress government, said, "Due to his credibility and experience in intelligence and security matters, Doval holds a greater influence than previous national security advisers." Patil said that there was a rumour for a long time that Doval had advised Modi even before he was elected prime minister in 2014.

In an August 2015 statement, Doval said, "India has the mindset that wherever it hits, it punches below its weight. We have to increase our weight and punch in the same proportion."

❑

12

Ajit Doval's Power Theory

We have not seen much clarity in Indian strategic thinking, despite the changing governments. But perhaps that is changing now. National Security Adviser Ajit Doval spoke on 'Security of State, The Art of Governance and Conflict of Values' in Mumbai recently and he said, "India has a mindset of punching below its weight. We must not punch below our weight or above our weight, but we should improve our weight and punch proportionately."

This is a simple, if not original, statement about the importance of running government effectively, despite indulging in speculation from time to time about the true nature of power. Some Indians may have rarely imagined in the more than 5,000 years of civilisation's history, that India will be a safer place in the long run if Doval and his boss Narendra Modi translate this principle into strategic thinking and purposeful action at the grassroots.

Among other things, Doval clearly pointed out that weak states invite trouble rather than mitigate or combat it. "If you are the instigator, you are partially responsible. But if you are not able to use the power, then you do not have it." This is again evident to all those who substitute emotions for clear thinking and especially those pacifists, who believe in lighting candles at Wagah or making unilateral concessions that will bring peace to India's relations with Pakistan. This is foolish from Pakistan's point of view, but will not do much for the security of Indians.

Doval also made an important distinction between individual morality and the actions of the state. A person can adopt non-violence and accept non-violence as a personal principle, but a nation cannot. Nations have to act for the greater good and a 'nation must resort to all means to defend itself.'

Doval said, "The first duty of the Government of India is to protect our country. Conflict of interest is automatic in this protection... When a nation acts judiciously within the boundaries of due process of law, its actions are right and it does not turn you into murderers."

We have allowed all power-related issues to degenerate into issues of personal morality and in the process have reduced ourselves to an ineffective and weak nation. We are paying the price for it recurrently.

The Abrahamic religions and Indian religions such as Hinduism, Buddhism and Jainism, asked themselves an important question about power and its permanence. They came to the opposite conclusion. Both recognised the transient nature of personal power. Eventually, we all die and are powerless to change our destiny; but the conclusions that we draw from this realisation have made a huge difference to our approach.

Indian philosophers viewed power as momentary and decided that the only power is the power over oneself as it directly affects the quality of our lives internally and externally. Thus, we became 'seekers' of truth instead of 'believers' in absolute truth. We have developed a two-pronged attitude towards power and we are still uncomfortable with its acquisition and use for temporary purposes. So, our emphasis on meditation, the victory over the ego, the individual religion—all these empower us spiritually; but we leave it naked when confronted with the external, physical force of our enemies.

The West saw the power and its transient nature and saw the need to make it lasting. They developed laws and institutions to uphold power beyond a lifetime.

The truth is not that the West was right and we were wrong, but that both ways are needed. Today, if the West adopts yoga and meditation as lifestyle options, it is because they see the futility of money and power, and an empty and meaningless life. On the contrary, we have to learn the lesson as to how to harness real power for the long-term benefit of society without losing our faith in inner spiritual development.

Our failure to find a balance between power over ourselves and long-term state power has resulted in our adopting soft choices and temporary non-solutions as an alternative to strategy and long-term thinking. I am, of course over-simplifying, because it is not true that Indian philosophers and empire-builders did not seek this balance (*Chanakya Niti* is an example of the kind of thought that seeks to create ideals by harnessing the various elements of power to form the state);

but the overall failure to harness the power and put it to good use is very visible in Indian history and continues to this day.

This is still evident today in our vigilance about the acquisition of economic and military power and in our tendency to confuse arguments about power with arguments for personal morality.

Gandhi described this approach as the best. He considered Jesus' Sermon on the Mount—a sermon to the defeated, which praised the virtues of humility as their guiding principle. Nehruvian policies, high moral principles and low capacity to live up to them are a direct result of Gandhi's principles.

Gandhi's advice to the victims of Hitler's aggression was something like this—leave yourself at his mercy, don't fight, rather, conquer the fascist dictator through love and peace-loving activities. Winston Churchill had better ideas than the ultra-moralistic Gandhi. It is not right to say that Gandhi was wrong, but advice, which may be absolutely right for an individual to apply to himself, may not be correct when applied thoughtlessly to others or to society as a whole. Personal morality, which results in failure (or success) affecting only one person can lead to disaster when it is applied to the society or the state.

Dr B.R. Ambedkar is cited in Arun Shourie's book to show how intrinsically focused Buddhism failed to note the threat of Muslim invaders and their symbolic fervour. In one stroke, the invaders destroyed all Buddhist monasteries and Buddha statues, bringing an end to the religion. Passivity and lack of real power played a decisive role in eliminating Buddhism from its native land.

Nothing illustrates our own current self-defeating attitudes towards power and morality better than the arguments we have heard about the death penalty. Those who want to abolish the death penalty like to quote Gandhi's statement that an eye for an eye and a tooth for a tooth will make the whole world blind and toothless.

Gandhi clearly did not understand game theory and the practical consequences of his personal morality. What may be true for individual violence may not be true for society and the state. If I hit you in the eye and you hit me back and I break your teeth and you hit me back, we can both become blind and toothless; but the same does not happen with the larger society when such a policy is followed. When an eye for an eye and a tooth for a tooth—both action and reaction continue for some time between two opposing societies or their respective kingdoms, both begin to act more cautiously. Both states go on to save themselves from being blind or toothless. Thus, the eyes and teeth are better protected and over time, both realise that there is no benefit in hitting the other's eye or breaking his teeth. In short, mutual power creates mutual resistance over time and leads to lasting peace.

This was clearly established in the 1980s through game theory experiments by Robert Axelrod at the University of Michigan. Axelrod invited game theorists to submit strategies for testing in computer-simulated games to test whether being a saint was a substitute for being sensible. His experiments sought to establish whether opponents tried to cooperate or deceive when they were unclear about the other person's true intentions. To make a long story short (you can read a summary of his experiments here), the strategy that won more often was 'tit for tat', meaning all players must try good faith the first time. But if the opponent plays dirty, you pay him back in the same coin. Over time, players can learn to cooperate.

The Gandhian argument of becoming blind and toothless is valid only in the individual context where victory and defeat can be defined by each individual. On the other hand, the inability to counterattack in a social or national context would actually invite attacks as Nehru found out with the Chinese in 1962 and as we have found time and again in treating Pakistan as a child. A strong state capable of giving as much as it receives is a prerequisite for peace.

Now consider what the true heirs think of Jesus' Sermon on the Mountain? How do they actually act contrary to what they say? No country with a Christian majority—from America to Britain—no member of the European Union will ever turn the other cheek when hit. Did George Bush turn the other cheek after 9/11? He hit hard twice. Does Israel believe in rolling on the ground when punched or giving it back in double measure? They retaliate. They fight. They try to win. No Muslim state will ever talk of peace if it feels it has been wronged, whether it is real or imagined.

The reason is simple: The West has learned to separate personal morality from state morality. The individual Christian may be ready to feed the lions in pursuit of his moral ideals, but he will never throw his citizens to the outside lions for the sake of the peace of the state.

The West's answer to the transient nature of power was to build a strong state not through individuals but through laws and institutions. This is an important lesson for us. A strong state places laws and institutions above the individual and can thus act altruistically in practice. A weak state would be truly tyrannical as it cannot be held responsible for failing to do its job. After all, it remains weak by definition.

Only a strong state can use power wisely and punch with its true weight. Weakness equals immorality when it comes to the state.

❑

13
The Inside Story of Doklam Success

Intense talks continued between the national security advisers of India and China—quietly and away from public glare through telephone lines as well as diplomatic efforts to resolve the crisis.

National Security Adviser Ajit Doval met his Chinese counterpart State Councillor Yang Jiechi in Beijing on the sidelines of the BRICS meeting on July 27–28, 2017, and held discussions on the crisis. Along with diplomatic efforts to resolve the crisis, conversations between the two national security advisers continued on telephone lines away from the glare of the public.

Chinese President Xi Jinping and Prime Minister Modi had decided that NSA Doval and his Chinese counterpart Yang Jiechi would talk to de-escalate tensions. NSA Doval and his counterpart met in Hamburg and had a long meeting. Further movement took place during the Beijing meeting. Foreign Secretary S. Jaishankar and Indian ambassador to Beijing Vijay Gokhale took the issue forward.

Later, China agreed not to build further roads in the Doklam area and to withdraw its troops from there.

Indian and Chinese troops had a heated standoff in Doklam since June 16 after Indian troops prevented Chinese forces from building a road in the disputed area. The Indian Army's tough stand in the standoff also helped to put pressure on China, which understood that India would not back down so easily without China acceding to its demands.

China finally agreed to completely withdraw its troops from the region. It was described as a major victory for Modi's national security team, including both civil and military diplomacy. External Affairs Minister Sushma Swaraj had said that both sides should first withdraw their troops before any talks and support a peaceful resolution of the border standoff.

On account of the standoff in Doklam, relations between the two countries had come to a lower level. The Chinese side had refused to back down. Beijing had accused India of infiltrating its territory and demanded the immediate withdrawal of Indian troops. The Chinese side, particularly the state media there, had been aggressive since then and had issued veiled threats of war on several occasions.

India maintained that the two sides should simultaneously back down before any talks on the issue, saying that war was not a solution. During the Doklam standoff, Ajit Doval proved that no diplomat is needed to resolve the international crisis. In de-escalation of the Doklam issue, it has been proved that diplomacy is an option to resolve crises of any magnitude.

The long haul of aggressive and outright psychological warfare waged by China did not seem to be coming to an end as its propaganda machinery continued its propaganda, threatening India with dire consequences. New Delhi was reminded of the 1962 defeat. The state media there was frenzied and its statements had a belligerent tone. It seemed from the tone that 'war' was imminent if the Indians did not withdraw from Doklam. The temperature was rising. There was no solution on the horizon and the ice seemed impossible to melt.

However, diplomatic efforts on India's part to end the standoff did not stop, especially ahead of the BRICS summit that began on September 3 in China. It must be said without exaggeration that there was one man who worked tirelessly and almost single-handedly to overcome the impasse. Relief came on 28 August and Indian and (later) Chinese forces began to retreat. The Ministry of External Affairs issued a statement and things progressed positively at an alarming pace. How did this happen?

The light was shining when it seemed that there was no light at the end of the tunnel. The withdrawal of troops was not easy at all, yet it happened. The person who led the team and took this forward was none other than India's National Security Adviser Ajit Doval. Amazingly, he is no diplomat by training or profession. He is an outstanding leader of men, who not only led from the front but also took everyone along. Insiders say that Doval, with a genius quality of inspiring his colleagues and esprit de corps, took a mission that appeared feasible and turned it into a 'mission accomplished'.

Let us quickly recap the events that led to this resolution. To prevent any further developments, Prime Minister Narendra Modi and Chinese President Xi Jinping decided to depute NSAs from both countries. Doval met with Yang Jiechi in Beijing and things began to escalate at a rapid pace, resulting in the decision to start separating the two armies as quickly as possible.

The Chinese ambassador in New Delhi was met shortly afterwards and the necessary dynamics for the Indian side were worked out. Showing his administrative acumen, skilful diplomatic tact and vision, Doval brought all the concerned people to the same table. Such tasks are not only difficult but also impossible. Doval proved useful with his immense experience and skilful negotiation in matters of statecraft. As a police officer, he is known for his quick temper. His masterstroke as an intelligence officer in bringing Mizo leader Laldenga to the table for the signing of the Mizo Accord and his remarkable vision and courageous acts during the peak of the Khalistan crisis certainly served as relevant experiences.

With clarity on the do's and don'ts during the delicate task of separation, Doval was extremely careful in implementing his blueprint while involving the army chief, heads of external and internal intelligence agencies and other need-based stakeholders with caution to bring them together on the same page for concrete action. The margin of error had to be zero and time was of the essence as the clock was ticking before the BRICS convention. China also wanted India not to skip the summit as it had done during the OBOR (One Belt One Road) meeting.

Another important nation that needed to be handled tactfully was Bhutan. Thimphu had to be managed with meticulous precision and finesse as the Himalayan kingdom was wary of Chinese edicts and did not want to be a scapegoat in the worst-case scenario.

In fact, the entire country heaved a sigh of relief after this separation as there was uncertainty as to whether the situation would worsen or deteriorate and turn into war. The signals were worrying because of two major factors—first, India had fought a war with China in the past, and second, the statements from both the 'warring' sides were intimidating. Electronic media was also beating the drums of war. Pakistan was watching which direction the wind was blowing—perhaps taking pleasure in the escalating tensions between China and India.

But many sceptics who made claims about the war were proved wrong. As they rightly say, 'prudence is the better part of valour'. With the de-escalation of tension over the Doklam issue, it was proved that diplomacy is an option to resolve a crisis of any magnitude and Doval has proved this adage.

It also proved beyond doubt that one does not need to be a professional diplomat, politician, party worker or international mediator to solve such a problem.

What is Doklam Dispute?

Doklam is a plateau, between the Ha Valley of Bhutan, East Sikkim district of India, and Yadong County, China. It is a trijunction, where the borders of India, China and Bhutan meet. This trijunction is just 15 km away from Nathu La Pass in India. Doklam is considered by both Bhutan and China as their territory. India considers Doklam a part of Bhutan.

Cause of dispute

To understand what is the Doklam dispute, one has to understand the intentions of China. China is an expansionist country. Under this expansionist thought process, China has ongoing disputes with almost all its neighbouring countries. In 1988 and 1998, there was an agreement between China and Bhutan that both countries would work towards maintaining peace in the Doklam region. Since 1988, circumventing this agreement, China has been encroaching on some areas of Bhutan. But there was no permanent presence of the Chinese People's Liberation Army in Doklam so far. For the first time, China began the construction of a flat road from Doklam to the Bhutan Army camp in Joomli. Bhutan has not been able to oppose this road construction militarily, although it has expressed its opposition several times through the ground and diplomatic channels with the Chinese side that the construction of the road inside Bhutanese territory is in violation of the earlier agreements.

Currently, the standoff between India and China on Doklam began when around 300 Indian soldiers with two bulldozers blocked the People's Liberation Army (PLA) of China from building a road in Doklam on 18 June 2017.

Why is India involved in this dispute?

Essentially, India has no claim in this region. Actually, there is a dispute between China and Bhutan regarding this area. A treaty was signed between India and Bhutan in the year 1949, in which it was decided that India would guide the foreign policy and defence matters of its neighbouring country Bhutan. Another agreement on military cooperation was signed between India and Bhutan in the year 2007. Article 2 of this agreement states—"In view of the close relations of friendship and cooperation between Bhutan and India, the government of Bhutan and the government of India shall cooperate with each other on issues relating to their national interests."

Cause of concern for India

Situated in the Chumbi Valley, Doklam is strategically important for India and China. As mentioned in the statement of the Ministry of External Affairs, the construction of the road by China will significantly change the current situation in the area. India considers this a violation of a mutual agreement signed in the year 2012. This is a matter of serious concern for the security of India. China will get a huge military advantage over India by building the road. The major reason for this is that if there is a smooth movement of China till Doklam, then China will have an edge over the 20 kilometre wide area connecting India with the north-eastern states. In Indian Army parlance, this area is called 'Chicken Neck'. In the event of war, China will get the benefit of capturing Doklam and Siliguri and its surrounding areas will come under China's control. If China deploys its artillery in Doklam, then India's chicken neck area will come under its control, which will pose an imminent danger of cutting off of the rest of India from the Northeast.

What is the History of Doklam?

China, which reminds us of history on all controversial issues, gives a similar argument on the Doklam issue. According to China, the name Doklam was used by Tibetan shepherds as an old pasture. China also claims that before 1960, Bhutanese shepherds used to go to Doklam with its permission, although there is no historical evidence of this.

What is the Current Status of the Doklam Issue?

The Doklam dispute, which went on for nearly 70 days, was resolved on August 28. After the ongoing diplomatic talks between the two countries, it was agreed to withdraw the forces.

On 16 June, the Indian Army stopped the Chinese Army by moving ahead in the disputed Doklam area to stop the Chinese Army's attempt to unilaterally change the status quo in this triangular border area by building a road. After this standoff, the armies of both the countries withdrew on August 28 and thus the situation before June 16 was restored.

Bhutan saw this move of the Chinese Army as an attempt by China to annex its land and the Bhutanese soldiers who were driven out by the Chinese soldiers called the Indian Army for help. India had challenged the Chinese Army on the basis of the defence agreement between India and Bhutan.

A Big Diplomatic Victory

This is certainly a diplomatic victory for India. The settlement of this dispute will help in establishing regional security and peace. The atmosphere became quite tense due to the continuous threat of war from the Chinese side, but India continued to maintain restraint on its part. India kept diplomatic options open. This helped in settling the dispute.

India and China's Argument on Doklam

China's claim: China has described Doklam as its area instead of the disputed site. It says that India has questioned its sovereignty by stopping construction there.

Indian side: When China started building a road in Doklam, Bhutan asked the Indian Army for help. Doklam is part of Bhutan and is a trijunction, where no change can take place without the consent of the three parties.

International viewpoint about Doklam

America

The US said that the status quo should be restored at the trijunction of the borders of the three countries. In this way, it opposed China's road construction.

Japan

Japan openly came out in support of India on the Doklam dispute. On threats from China, the ambassador of Japan to India said that no one should change the status quo by using force.

Bhutan

China spread the lie that Bhutan has accepted Doklam as part of China. But Bhutan's foreign ministry immediately said that building the road there was a clear violation of treaties.

Nepal

Nepal's Deputy Prime Minister Krishna Bahadur Mahara said that Nepal will not take any sides in the border dispute. India and China should find a solution peacefully.

Pakistan

On 18 July, Pakistani media claimed that the Chinese Army launched an attack in Doklam and killed 158 Indian soldiers. Pakistan was exposed due to this false news.

Doklam Tension: Events

On June 16, Doklam became the cause of tension between India and China when China tried to build a road there. That was opposed by the Indian Army.

June 18: Indian forces cross this border and stop the road construction work going on there.

June 19: India accuses China of trying to violate the peace agreement by building a road in Doklam. China accuses India of crossing its border.

June 20: Ambassador of Bhutan registers a protest against Chinese incursions into its territory.

June 23: China halts the first batch of Indian pilgrims on way to the Kailash Mansarovar Yatra.

June 28: Army Chief General Bipin Rawat visits Sikkim and takes stock of the situation at the Doklam trijunction.

June 29: China tests a 35-tonne military tank near the Nathu La border.

June 30: Defence Minister Arun Jaitley says, "China should now know that today's India is very different from 1962." China says, "China is also not the China of 1962."

July 6: China postpones the meeting of Prime Minister Narendra Modi and Chinese President Xi Jinping to be held at the G-20 summit.

July 20: Chinese media threatens war and says 'Hindu nationalism' has influenced Prime Minister Narendra Modi's China policy.

July 20: External Affairs Minister Sushma Swaraj says, "India wants to resolve the border dispute with China through dialogue. For this, both countries will have to withdraw their forces from Doklam first."

July 27: National Security Adviser (NSA) Ajit Doval holds talks with Chinese NSA and State Counsellor Yang Jiechi on the side-lines of the meeting of top security officials of BRICS countries.

August 2: The Chinese foreign ministry, citing a letter written by Jawaharlal Nehru to Zhou En-Lai on March 22, 1959, in support of the agreement reached at the Anglo-Chinese

Conference of 1890, has said that neither Bhutan nor India have a claim on Doklam.

August 8: Defence Minister Arun Jaitley says, "India's forces are ready for any kind of war."

August 10: Bhutan rejects China's statement that Doklam is a part of China. It was claimed by the Chinese foreign ministry that Bhutan had agreed to accept that Doklam fell in the Sikkim sector as part of China.

August 15: Chinese forces try to infiltrate Indian territory on the northern bank of Pangong Lake. After failing, the Chinese soldiers started pelting stones. China says that it has no knowledge of the incident.

❑

14

Head of Strategic Policy Group

The Modi government set up a Strategic Policy Group (SPG) to assist the National Security Council and help in the long-term strategic defence review. According to a top Home Ministry official, the panel is the key mechanism for inter-ministerial coordination and integration of relevant inputs in the formulation of national security policies.

The SPG is headed by National Security Adviser Ajit Doval and its members include the vice chairman of NITI Aayog, the cabinet secretary, the chiefs of the three defence services, the RBI governor, the foreign secretary, the home secretary, the finance secretary, and the defence secretary. The secretary, Department of Defence Production and Supplies, scientific adviser to the defence minister and secretary, Cabinet Secretariat are also members of the panel.

Other members are—the secretary, Revenue Department; secretary, Department of Atomic Energy; secretary, Department of Space; director, Intelligence Bureau; and secretary, National Security Council Secretariat. According to another official, if needed, representatives of other ministries and departments could be invited to the group meetings.

The national security adviser convenes the meetings of the SPG and the cabinet secretary coordinates the implementation of the decisions of the group by the central ministries and departments and the state governments.

The panel makes National Security Adviser Ajit Doval the most powerful bureaucrat in India since the post was created in 1998.

❑

15

The Threat of Terrorism and Capability to Respond

Causality proves correlation, but correlation does not prove causality. The absence of any major incident after 26/11 is correlated with terrorism, but its absence does not prove the disappearance of the threat. Event-centred assessments often lead to such simplifications because the human mind is designed to simplify complex issues so as to bring them within the limits of comprehension.

During a 'Security Summit' at the battered Trident Hotel in Mumbai on November 14, 2009, Maharashtra's director general of police claimed that 'the police response mechanism has improved significantly and we are now much more confident'. It is a matter of happiness. But it should be taken with a pinch of salt.

A statement issued earlier this year by Mustafa Abu-al-Yazid, one of Al-Qaeda's top functionaries, is said to have claimed that the 'The Islamic State which gave birth to the brave and heroic martyrs of Bombay, who killed you in your home and humiliated you, is capable of producing thousands more like them'. This is a tall claim, not a measure of their true abilities. No one can bet their money except speculators where there is truth. It calls for a professional approach rather than a crystal gaze.

For meaningful risk assessment changes, if any, the two independent factors that determine the security quotient need to be analysed. The first pertains to the 'provocative', that is, the outline of the source of the threat. Changes in threat level are largely determined by changes in the potential and intentions of the threat source. The second is related to 'response', i.e. the ability of the threatened entity to destroy, prevent or stop the threat.

As assessed in the light of revelations made by David Headley and Tahawur Rana, HUJI and Lashkar-e-Taiba activists targeting the Indian High Commission in Dhaka in Bangladesh, investigations into counterfeit Indian currency cases which indicate ISI linkages, continued infiltration and attacks in Jammu and Kashmir, from the revelations made by jihadis arrested from different parts of the country, etc., it is evident that the threats from terrorist groups and their masters are not reducing.

Although intentions remain unchanged and capabilities remain intact, there have been two changes in the past year that will affect Pakistan's ability to convert its diabolical intentions into action on the ground. First, violent insurgency using terrorism as its strategy, and second, Pakistan is coming under heavy international scrutiny on the terrorism front, making it difficult to operate with impunity as in the past.

Contrary to a simple assessment, these factors do not reduce the threat, but may change its character to the detriment of India. The new schemes will be more devious and cautious and will try to leave no trail of involvement. This would give Pakistan more autonomy to act without withholding resources to groups enjoying its patronage—a freedom that could hurt India. Also, wrongly suspecting India to be responsible for its woes, it can ask Lashkar, HUJI, HM, etc., to retaliate. Since the operational capabilities of these organisations are intact and so are their striking capabilities, it would be incorrect to assume that the changed setting would reduce the threat level.

According to Musharraf, "ISI always gains entry in every group and that is the efficiency, effectiveness of ISI. You should have access so that you can influence all the organisations and use them for the benefit of Pakistan."

Recent moves indicate future use with greater tactical vigilance and diligence, such as operations through the bases in a third country, recruitment of local youth for operations, expansion of the network in smaller towns, providing sleeper cells with ostensible cover, issuing strict instructions to Lashkar, HUJI and others on communication, etc. The dangers have not diminished, but are changing their character.

During the last one year, some changes have been made mainly to address the shortcomings of the past. Should there be a repeat of Mumbai? The Indian response should be better. Introduction of rapid response teams, acquisition of latest weapons, redeployment of National Security Guard (NSG), formation of National Investigation Agency (NIA), provision of combat vehicles equipped with the latest weapons and global positioning system (GPS), etc., in some high vulnerability areas will give momentum. Improved firepower and strategic advantage to our forces will add advantage although the defence of vulnerable targets has also been strengthened with better technological support in limited areas.

However, given India's size, diversity and independence, the country cannot be defended only in a defensive mode. The cases of Headley and Rana are indicative of an affordable shortfall in our armour.

The nation's security levels cannot be raised unless the capability of terrorist groups is reduced, their allied ties with gun wielders, financiers and the underworld dismantled, sleeper cells dismantled and the ground support bases destroyed through a planned and sustained effort.

Not much has been achieved, though. Rather, the capabilities have not been built to meet these goals. India cannot depend for its security on the expectation that adversaries fall prey to their own contradictions or take foreign initiatives to reduce threats to India. New threats may approach us in those areas where we are least prepared and in the forms we least expect and the country has not prepared itself yet.

❑

16

Abolition of Article 370 and Ajit Doval

The trio of Prime Minister Narendra Modi, Home Minister Amit Shah and National Security Adviser Ajit Doval abolished Article 370 in such a neat manner that no one even got to know about it. In this Mission Kashmir of the Modi government, NSA Ajit Doval played the role of James Bond in a true sense. If there has been no violence so far after the removal of Article 370 in Kashmir, then the credit for this goes to Home Minister Amit Shah, who formulated the strategy for the removal of Article 370 as well as Ajit Doval who prepared the ground for the same in Kashmir, who once again proved his ability to the country.

After the removal of Article 370, Ajit Doval said, "I am absolutely sure that most of the Kashmiri people support the removal of Article 370. They are seeing more and more economic progress, their bright future and employment opportunities. Only some crooked tendencies are opposing it."

Ajit Doval added, "There is no question of the army's atrocities there. Only the state police and some central forces maintain law and order. The Indian Army is there to fight terrorists."

Further, he said, "92.5 per cent of the geographical area of Jammu and Kashmir is free from restrictions." On the preventive detention of state leaders, he said, "They have been kept in preventive custody as there could be problems in maintaining law and order if there are gatherings and terrorists would use the situation to their advantage."

He also observed, "No leader of Jammu and Kashmir has been charged with criminal case or sedition. They have been kept in custody till the situation returns to normal." At the same time, he also said, that it has been done as per the law. Doval affirmed, “I think the situation in Jammu and Kashmir is getting much better than what I anticipated. Only one incident has been reported—on August 6, in which a young boy succumbed to his injuries. He didn't die of a shot. The post-mortem report states that he died due to injuries inflicted by some heavy object.”

After the removal of Article 370 from Jammu and Kashmir, National Security Adviser Ajit Doval also met ordinary Kashmiris and discussed their problems. He assured people that ‘keeping your children safe is our priority’. He said, “Your safety is our responsibility.” While interacting with common Kashmiris, Ajit Doval also shared a meal with them.

National Security Adviser Ajit Doval also met personnel of paramilitary forces deployed in the valley. He boosted their morale. He also met the soldiers of the Jammu and Kashmir Police and boosted their morale. Ajit Doval kept a very close watch on the situation in the valley after the removal of Article 370.

Doval reassured the people, “Everything will be fine. Your safety and security are our responsibility.” Meanwhile, unprecedented security measures were taken in Kashmir and several restrictions were imposed and all communication services were suspended to maintain law and order. Doval was seen eating food and talking to locals on a footpath outside closed shops. He exchanged views with the people on the security issue and the government's decision to remove Article 370 and bifurcate the state into two union territories. The national security adviser told the people, "You and your children will live here. They will make a name for themselves in the world."

He also met the police personnel present in the area and appreciated their role in keeping the situation under control in the state for the past several years. Doval told the policemen, "Jammu and Kashmir Police is one of the best police forces. It has a special place for us." Later, the video of Doval talking to local people and policemen went viral on social media. He was accompanied by state director general of police, Dilbagh Singh.

It should be noted that the central government abolished Article 370 which gave special status to Jammu and Kashmir and by passing the Jammu and Kashmir Reorganisation Bill, divided it into two parts and declared it as a union territory. One part is Jammu and Kashmir, which will have an assembly, while the other part will be Ladakh, which will be a union territory without a legislature.

During his visit to the valley, National Security Adviser Ajit Doval ensured that there was no loss of life and property in the valley. He interacted with the local people in Shopian and had food with them. The area was once notorious for terrorist activities.

A video of Doval surfaced on social media. In this, Doval was seen telling the local people that once the new administration takes over, everything would change.

On August 5, 2019, the government withdrew the special status of Jammu and Kashmir. Article 370 was nullified. Jammu and Kashmir and Ladakh were declared to be converted into union territories. Ajit Doval continued to review the security arrangements by reaching Jammu and Kashmir even before the announcement of the abrogation of Article 370. After the removal of Article 370, the national security adviser took stock of the situation in the entire Srinagar city, Pulwama, Awantipora, Pampore and Budgam amid tension in the Valley.

It is noteworthy that Ajit Doval remained the eyes and ears of the central government in Jammu and Kashmir and kept a close watch on the situation. Ajit Doval is said to have nationalist views and Prime Minister Modi has unflinching faith in him. Ajit Doval is not only the national security adviser in the Modi government, he has also been given cabinet status this time over.

The prayers for Eid-al-Adha were performed peacefully in mosques on Monday morning in Kashmir Valley on Eid, August 12, 2019. But due to restrictions like curfew, the festivities were missing on the streets. National Security Adviser Ajit Doval conducted a recce of the entire Srinagar city, Pulwama and Awantipora districts of South Kashmir, besides Pampore and Budgam on the day. Eid was celebrated peacefully in all the areas.

Doval was personally seen talking to the local people at the grassroots level and convincing them that his only option was India and its development model. Radical Islamic Wahhabi Salafism, which incites youth under the guise of political jihad, is India's major concern.

Doval camped in the valley for 11 days after the announcement of the abolition of the special status of the state. After the government's decision, the NSA toured from the downtown Srinagar to the militancy-hit Shopian district of South Kashmir in order to avoid any untoward situation and to maintain people's confidence in the government.

On the occasion of Eid-al-Adha, more than 10,000 people offered prayers in mosques of

Jammu and Kashmir on the day of Bakri-Eid peacefully. According to the information, residents of Anantnag, Baramulla, Budgam and Bandipora offered *namaz* and distributed sweets. No untoward incident was reported in Jammu and Kashmir during that period.

During that time, Doval also met sheep vendors and interacted with them. A lot was at stake for Doval, individually, and for the government collectively. Section 144 remained in force in the state. The government achieved a major political and diplomatic victory by breaking the contact of the local population with Pakistan.

❑

17

Afghan Crisis and Ajit Doval

India hosted top security officials from Russia, Iran and five Central Asian countries for a discussion regarding security during the Afghanistan crisis. All officials explored the shared vision for practical cooperation in combating the growing menace of terrorism, radicalisation and drug abuse in the aftermath of the Afghan crisis. China was invited to the 'Delhi Regional Security Dialogue on Afghanistan', but it had already informed India that it would be unable to attend the meeting owing to some issues related to the timing of the programme. Pakistan also decided not to attend the meeting.

Top security officials from Kazakhstan, Kyrgyzstan, Tajikistan, Turkmenistan and Uzbekistan attended the discussion which was chaired by National Security Adviser Ajit Doval. The security complexities in the post-Taliban occupation of Afghanistan were discussed among the eight countries that attended the meeting. And the talks mainly focused on collaborating on practical issues to deal with the challenges.

NSA Ajit Doval affirmed, "I am confident that our discussions will contribute to helping the Afghan people and enhancing our collective security. Recent developments in Afghanistan have important implications not only for the people of that country but also for its neighbours and the region."

Presiding over the meeting, Doval noted in his inaugural address, "It is time for closer discussions, greater cooperation and coordination among regional countries on the Afghan situation. We are all closely monitoring developments in that country."

However, after Pakistan, China also refused to attend the NSA meeting to be held in Delhi on November 10 on the issue of Afghanistan.

Responding as to why it did not attend the meeting, China said that it was unable to attend because of 'scheduling issues'. At the same time, sources said that China had conveyed to India that it was prepared for both multilateral and bilateral talks with India on the issue of Afghanistan.

❑

18

India is Set to Become a Superpower: Doval

A lot has been said about Sardar Patel's great contribution and his efforts to unite the country. But above all, he was a great visionary. He was a visionary who could think far ahead of his time and imagine what harm could have been brought about if he did not take the steps he eventually did. Perhaps it would not have mattered if the sovereignty of India had not been established during his lifetime. But if it had not happened after his lifetime, it would have become a cause of terrible disintegration for the country. He united this country. When we imagine the future, there are two aspects involved in it—one is that what you see in your future, which is based on your practical experience or past experience. You think not only of your generation but also of the generations to come, and then your vision has a direction. Perhaps vision without a direction has no meaning, so farsightedness is very important in nation-building. This is similar to the role of radar in a missile or in the advanced aircraft we use today; and this vision or farsightedness, which does not stop at that person or even generation, is a continuous process. If a country has to become great, then everyone should have a vision and only that creates a broad vision of a country.

How many of you remember what was China's situation in the late 1970s? It was far behind India. It hardly had defence industries and technical capability. We had a setback in 1962, but we cannot gauge the real situation from that. India was far ahead of China then. But there was one person—Deng Xiaoping, who had a vision. That vision extended till 2050 and in that, he had envisioned how China has to emerge as the world's superpower, what China should do, so that by 2010 it becomes world's big economic power, what should it do to become an industrial power by the end of the last century, how can it become a major military power by 2020, and how should it avoid all major military conflicts till 2050 till it starts leading the world. It was this vision that transformed China.

Today, the world is excited about India. You see the statements of leaders, academicians, strategic thinkers, international institutions and global media. All of them are full of possibilities and hopes for India. India stands on the threshold of a wonderful journey. Perhaps this enthusiasm is not because they are well-wishers of India, but in the rise of India lies the interest of the whole world. The emergence of India as a pluralistic free democracy means many things to the world. There is a question that is very important and which is frequently asked about the rise of China. Will the rise of China be peaceful? No one asks this question about India. Sometimes it is asked whether India will be able to take advantage of this opportunity or will it miss this opportunity as people feel that such big opportunities were frequently repeated in India's long journey, but India missed them. It had the ability to do it, but it could not. Why do they think that this time India can do it? Why is there this mood of elation, this enthusiasm, now, in the whole world?

Undoubtedly one of our greatest strengths is our stable democratic constitutional polity. Our free pluralistic society is run according to the law. What is associated with this is our fastest growing 'economy', our population and the power of our youth. India will remain the youngest country in the world by 2065. So, we have a long time when the world's leading manpower and youth power will come from this country. But the most important thing is that Indian politics has been able to bring effective leadership in front of the country. A government, which came with an absolute majority, has been successful in changing the direction of progress and development. There is no doubt about the world's estimate that by 2030, India will become the third-largest economy in the world. It will become an economy of more than 11 trillion. It will be the third superpower after the US and China. Its military power will be such, perhaps the most capable military power, which will be able to bring stability not only in the region but also outside it. It is also realised that its technical cost will contribute to the core areas of technology, perhaps in space, cyber, nanotechnology, or even more advanced technology.

But are the people of India equally excited about it? Do you think their attitude is like that? I wanted to see how many articles have been written on the subject of where India will be by 2030. I found that most of them are sourced from outside countries. Some are copied and pasted and are mediocre work, but original thinking is not to be seen in India. We just don't have the attitude to have long-term strategic thinking. Maybe we lack confidence. We feel that everything is quite uncertain, it is a fantasy, and nothing like this is going to happen. I wonder why this is so? Why is the attitude of Indians like this? An argument has been made that this is due to the inertia created by the years of slavery, servitude and subjugation. You live in the present, live in today, my problem is how to survive today. What is distant for me is very scary. It raises great confusion and doubt. I'm not sure if I will be able to do that or not! Let me think about today; tomorrow will be taken care of tomorrow. So, one is the historical reason.

The second argument that has been made is that Indians are quite individualistic. This is a psychological reason. Psychologically you think of yourself, but vision is something that is collective, something in which you think ahead of yourself. In it, you think about your neighbour, your surroundings, your community, your country, and your society. But if you say that I hardly have the means and ability to take care of myself, then how can I think of others? If you have such an individualistic attitude, and if you want salvation, then you can go to the Himalayas and live in a hut in seclusion. You would like to acquire knowledge for yourself. It is not collective. You wouldn't want to pray together or even go to war together. Sikhism taught us, and Guru Gobind Singh realised that when you want to fight together, you have to eat together, worship together and stay together.

But perhaps there is one more thing, which is also somewhat painful, which I was reading about. Shri I.G. Patel had said that Indians do not dream and politicians are responsible for this. He said that they saw so many dreams, but those dreams never came true; so, they have lost faith in those dreams. They talk of a good tomorrow so that they get votes today, but that tomorrow never comes. Is this true? Let's talk about it fairly honestly. We don't need to humiliate ourselves. Do you know that in 1945, the population of India was 32 crores? We had the whole of Punjab, which later became West Pakistan, and the whole of Bangladesh, which was then East Bengal with a population of 320 million and these two regions guaranteed food for India. One used to grow wheat, the other rice, and then there was a famine. And do you know how many people died in that famine? Five lakh people died in that famine. I don't know how many people know about this! Nobody even talked about it. Those 5 lakh people could neither be buried nor burnt. The British asked the Indian Army to dig trenches and put the dead bodies in them. Perhaps our compatriots have forgotten this chapter of history. Today we are a country with a population of 130 crores and now there is neither that part of Punjab (which is now in Pakistan) nor that part of Bengal (which is now Bangladesh). Not only does every Indian have enough food today, but the export of excess produce creates a market for abundance. Agricultural land has shrunk. Do you think Indians have done nothing? Don't you think we should be proud of it? Perhaps in the last 70 years we have made progress in many ways. It takes many countries centuries to do that. We are in the cyber sector, in the space sector, in the technology sector and we have the best institutions and the best human resources. So, we don't need to curse ourselves. And don't stop dreaming just because some of your dreams didn't come true. Being associated with security, I consider it more important because when your dreams come true or you stop dreaming, then your intent becomes weak and when the country's intent becomes weak then it can never become a superpower. An army whose intent is destroyed can never fight. Wars are not fought to kill people. People are not murderers. Wars are fought to destroy the intent of the country against which we are fighting. So, it accepts the conditions of peace that we want. The war is fought to weaken the morale of that country and if we ourselves break the intent of our country with our negativity and apathy, then perhaps our future will not be good and this is the painful thing which the countrymen themselves do not realise. We should be proud of what the world is saying about India, but we do not recognise our strength. We cannot become great unless our society and our people think that it is within us and that we are capable of doing it and achieving it.

Now let me go back to my topic—what are the dangers? What are some hidden dangers that we have to avoid? First thing—avoid, oppose and fight anything that weakens the intent of the country. Build the strong will of the country and the country will be built automatically. There are many forces, more internal than external, which are bent upon weakening the intent of the country. We are very fortunate that the national will of the country has awakened in the last four years. It has become powerful. Today people are happy that wherever they go in the world, they can walk with their heads held high. They take pride in the many new endeavours that have been initiated and I would say that they are successful. All these experiments, improvements and all these efforts generate energy. They generate heat and so they hurt. No country can become big and great without a little suffering. We also have to make sacrifices for the generations to come. Do not forget that our previous generations, who did not live to see the happy results of freedom, made many sacrifices. Since they suffered, can't we also suffer a bit? It is these hardships that will ensure that your children and their children will be able to live in a country where India will be respected more in the world than ever before, where India will have more power. India's destiny is very good.

If someone asks me what is India's biggest contribution in the last few years or what is India's biggest achievement, I would say that India has started realising its strength. It has started building up its national will and this national will is visible when we take a strong stand within and outside the country, when we pursue our independent foreign policy in the best interest of our country. Even when it comes to relations with the major powers, we are ready to defend Indian interests with full confidence, but for this there should be national will and will of the people. So, I think that the primary danger we have to avoid is that we should not let this national will weaken, but there are also other reasons why I decided to talk about it.

Right from childhood, we are taught to do good. If you do this, this will happen; eating this is good for your health. We are always told what we should do! That's why many people say that poverty should be eradicated, there should be urban development, better food, better health, better roads, as all these are very important. Since much has been said about this, I will not go into the details. Many of these things are already available. Then there's another point—the cost of negative factors in life, at least in terms of security, far outweighs the benefit of positive factors. If I do a hundred good things in life, but if I lose one battle, the loss will probably outweigh the victories in all the tactical battles that I have fought. You put your whole life into building a brand and a single mistake ruins everything. Hence, negative factors are important and so, don't underestimate them.

Often many countries fail, not because they can't do the right things, but because they did something that was wrong. Of course, there is a personal reason as well. Do you know what is the biggest contribution of a man's wife in his life? She stops him from making mistakes. She tells him what not to do. Perhaps he wants to be adventurous or take more risks, take more chances than others. But she acts as a brake. It's not as if she stops the car completely, but she slows it down and keeps it below the danger mark. So, just imagine; if Hitler had not attacked Russia, he would have won the Second World War. He made a mistake; I mean the whole of Europe was ruined because of what he did. He made just one mistake. If Mussolini had not invaded Greece, if Japan had not bombed Pearl Harbour, if the Soviets had not entered Afghanistan, if Nehru had not ignored Sardar Patel's advice on Kashmir, and if after the 1970 elections, after the 1970 National Assembly election in Pakistan, the Awami League, which had an absolute majority, had allowed Mujibur Rahman to become the prime minister, Bangladesh would not have been formed. Just one mistake. So, avoid mistakes.

But these mistakes, which are common as well as specific, are context-related. Today, I am talking about India. In the context of India, we have to assess India's own weaknesses, strengths, India's own threats and opportunities. Where can we go wrong in this regard? It's not as if it will be right or wrong for the rest of the future. I am looking at it over the next ten years. Avoid these mistakes for the next ten years. It is not as if after that there will be no need to be careful about mistakes. Mistakes may happen, but the references will be new. There will be a new India. The people, thinkers, analysts and strategists of that time will have to think again about their time. We have to think about what to avoid and what to do in the new context.

Let me tell you about a theory. It is basically a principle of security, but it is also a general principle. Your biggest strength is your insecurity. The lowest number of deaths by drowning is in Rajasthan. It is not that the people of Rajasthan are excellent swimmers, rather they do not attempt it. On the other hand, the highest number is in Kerala or in the coastal areas, where people are born swimmers. They start swimming in the sea from the age of three or four. If you are a billionaire, then you run the risk of losing billions, which is not the case with me. That's why it is your strength as well as a risk for you unless you are extremely careful with it. People can take away from you what you have.

Our biggest strengths are our democracy, and our politics, which are based on the Constitution. Our pluralistic society, the legacy of our great civilisation, and as Robinson, who did extensive research and wrote a book— *Why Nations Fail*, in which he wrote and I quote— 'Those who fail to ensure inclusive political, economic, social development tend to fail'. That is why it is very important that our democracy remains safe. There are many good things about it. Our Constitution, our institutions, our laws, they are all acceptable. But can this democracy be a weak democracy? Can this democracy lead us to 2030 as we envisage it? Yes, it can, if we can avoid some things and today, I am going to tell you about them. Since it is our greatest strength, it also has some inherent dangers. The first is that it can become a soft power. The weakness of democracy can make a country a soft power and India cannot afford to become a soft power for the next ten years. It has to be a soft power with all the attributes of soft power, but it also has to be a hard power because it will be forced to make tough decisions. You become a soft power when you make compromises and you make compromises when your political interests outweigh the interests of the country. Therefore, if India does not want to become a democracy that makes it a soft power, then there should be such governments in India that are stable, decisive, and who assume power with an absolute majority, that is, they get a full mandate. A minority government can delay or make it impossible to realise India's dreams because weak governments are unable to take tough decisions and it will be necessary to take tough decisions to take India forward—such tough decisions, which are in the interest of the public; but our decisions should not be populist.

The second problem is that of unstable governments, which are always at the risk of getting dismantled; corruption rises, and local and regional politics overshadow the larger interests and that is the threat. Do you want to hear examples? There was a time when Brazil developed very well. It was heading towards ultimate development. Do you know that when BRICS was formed, Brazil was an emerging country? But then what happened? It was making great progress under Lulu's government and then suddenly politics made it disintegrate and weaken and today Brazil is not only stagnant but it is declining. South Africa was developing well, but today we can see what is happening in South Africa. Greece was one of the founding countries of the United Nations. It was once a developed country. What happened to Greece? Politics of fragmentation, coalitions, unstable coalitions and collapse of governments. The development of Italy in Europe is also an example. You can see that democratic countries are powerful and effective in the world and democracy can also lead to a pluralistic and holistic development of the countries, provided that they do not make mistakes, and if people are alert, then they will not be weak.

Hence, India cannot afford the risk of unstable alliances. I do not know what the scenario after 2030 will be; but before that, we want a decision-making government, a decision-making leadership.

Second, I want to say that don't mistake democracy for the ballot box. The ballot box is a way to decide who will make laws for you and what will be the laws of this country. It is not democracy in itself. Democracy is when the laws made by the representatives of the people will be obeyed and implemented with full force. Democracy has no meaning if the government is not capable or refuses to implement those laws with full force. What's the use of laws that you can't enforce? What has happened is that we think that democracy survives as long as we have people's representatives in the executive or to make laws. We are not governed by the representatives of the people, rather we are governed by laws, which are made by the people's representatives. That is why the rule of law is very important. We must avoid any weakness in the rule of law. Sometimes I see such tendencies that we do not fully understand or realise that political convenience or corruption also undermines the rule of law. All temptations to undermine the rule of law should be avoided if a strong India is to emerge.

But there is another danger before democratic countries where misleading narratives destabilise a country and weaken democracy. In a democracy, the people have the right to choose. How do they choose? They make choices based on the information that reaches them and the data that reaches them. For example, there are four food items. I will choose which of them are favourable for my health based on the information given to me about the four dishes, and what if one of those four turns out to be poison? I have information that it is the nectar that will make me immortal; so, if I eat it, I may die. Democracy requires that the people should be knowledgeable, educated and well informed. They should be given the right information and get the right education. What if what is motivating you and influencing your decision is wrong and there is always the possibility of misrepresentation, which seeks to derail democracy? Today its expansion has increased manifold due to technology and it is the responsibility of every citizen, every media, every intellectual, every institution and every seminar that you go to, to weaken the power of this false propaganda. Misinformation is spread. I am told that there are agencies that specialise in just this kind of work. I have been told that there are different departments in intelligence agencies, which are engaged in fabricating deceptive news against their enemy countries and people fall into the trap. When I talk about hard power, which I will discuss in a while, I will talk about psychological warfare. Do you know how much effort the British had made against Germany during the Second World War to tell the German people that they were in danger and that they were about to be defeated? Even in those days, it had spent millions of pounds to spread misinformation and create an atmosphere against Hitler. I am not saying that what they did was wrong, but the fact is that it can influence people's thinking.

There is a very interesting story in the Mahabharata. It so happened that when the war of Mahabharata was about to start and Karna was appointed as the commander-in-chief of the Kaurava army, he needed a charioteer. Duryodhana said, "I cannot give you a better charioteer than Krishna. He is God himself." Karna said, "If I have to fight with Arjuna, I need a charioteer who can match his ability, but it is not possible. Suggest someone else." So, the second-best person available was Shalya, the king of Madra. Actually, he was a devotee of Lord Krishna, but he agreed when he was persuaded by Duryodhana. However, he had one condition. He said, "Once I get on your chariot, I should be allowed to talk to you whenever I want." So, it was agreed. Karna did not like that because he wanted to focus his attention on the war, yet he said that it was fine. When the war started, his charioteer affirmed, "Karna, your death is certain. You can never win. He is very powerful. Even the Lord is on his side." However, he continued to drive the chariot with great care as ordered by Karna. He did everything, but also kept trying to break his morale by talking continuously. Karna was so upset by this that when the chariot finally came face to face, he told him to leave the chariot. Shalya said, "Whether I stay or leave, your death is certain." What happened after that was the final chapter of the war.

Therefore, such deceptive things can have a great impact on the fate of a country. We have a habit of talking nonsense, talking irresponsibly. We think that it doesn't matter. This is a very silly idea. We write what we think about the reputation and respect of others, but if I have faith in something, an environment will be created wherein that trust will be shaken. You don't know how nation-building is carried out. For that, we should have unwavering faith in our Constitution, our law, the justice system, and everything else and strengthen it repeatedly. I am not saying that they are always right. Let go of those mistakes, but be positive about them. Communal riots, caste-related riots, or social enmity are created because of negativity and misinterpretation. A country can face many dangers where the public works on the basis of wrong statistics.

I believe that the second area of our strength is our economy and I think that the Indian economy is one of the biggest sources of strength for us today. The world considers us the fastest growing economy in the world and as I said, by 2030, we will occupy the third position. But believe me, it could go wrong, it could be messy. There are a few things we should avoid if we don't want it to be a mess. Populist measures should not be given more importance than national needs. It is greed. You refuse to take or do things that are in the interest of the country. For a short time, some people will suffer from them for a while. People will have problems. There are many things you can do to be popular among the people. But when you have to make sound decisions, tough decisions that are in the larger interest of the country, even if they are not very populist, and if you don't make them, perhaps the country will not be able to achieve its goal, it will not be able to realise its dream. If you don't have one tax system, one law, one system of governance in the whole country, then obviously the economy will not run well. It can only run a small economy, but when there is a big economy, there is a huge economy, when you talk about a 10–11 trillion economy, your tax system should not be so scattered.

If you have a 20 million economy, your tax structure and tax rate will be different; but some problems may arise if you take action for tax. You have the option to take populist decisions or take steps that are in the interest of the country. Therefore, we have to keep populist decisions secondary to decisions in the interest of the country. Under this comes the fiscal management of the economy. Sometimes some stringent steps have to be taken for fiscal management or budget preparation. Today, we are faced with a very difficult situation of inflation of crude oil all over the world. This is a time of crisis for us, it is also a time of crisis for many non-producing countries. But as a country, we have to see whether we can completely separate ourselves from the international prices. And make it populist by saying, 'We will give up everything else and subsidise it' or we will say, 'The country will bear the burden and we will divide it amongst ourselves.' This time shall pass. It is not in our power to reduce its prices. There may be some reduction in the next six months or eight months, but hopefully, the prices will stabilise. If we do not deviate from the path and issues, then the momentum of our growth will not be affected. But if we turn it into a populist decision for short-term gains, we may lose sight of that path of progress. So, we should move in that direction accordingly.

There is one more thing that I think not everyone would like to hear—that every Indian is a patriot. People who are in government alone do not have the monopoly to be patriots. I have seen that people from all walks of life and most of my colleagues from the media are patriotic. Not all private sectors are traitors. This country cannot be economically prosperous unless our private sector is strong. President Obama comes and addresses the parliament and says I'm taking a 10 billion order for my private sectors. We would be afraid to promote our private sectors by going to other countries in this manner. We should do this and if Indian corporates spread all over the world, then maybe it will be beneficial for us. See how China is promoting it; many countries in the world are promoting it as well. We had developed an attitude that if we do this, then maybe there is corruption involved. No, there is no corruption in this. The Government of India has a lot to do, but the Government of India is not a business establishment. It cannot be or replace corporate houses and we cannot have big corporate houses unless there is capital creation and capital creation cannot take place until profits are created. If there is no profit, then capital cannot be created; if there is no capital, then there will be no investment; if there is no investment, then employment will not be created; if employment is not created then revenue will not be created; if there is no revenue generation, then the government will have no money to spend, which is the goal anyway. Whatever money is spent on our army, our police, our defence, railways, communication, space, etc., is exorbitant. So, where is the money coming from? We cannot treat them as enemies. We have to change our mindset. The bad among them should be put behind bars. Strictest rules should be made for that; but by doubting everyone and creating an environment where they do not develop—inside and outside the country, then India will be able to develop only to a limited level. India's business houses and corporate houses have to be promoted if it has to rise above that level.

China is a communist country and you see how establishments like 'Ali Baba' have become big corporates and how much the Chinese government has supported them. Today, China's dominance in the world is not due to Chinese government companies, but because of private companies, which are almost government companies. We would also like our private companies to be like the companies of the Government of India. They should act according to India's strategic interests, follow them and promote them to the extent that it benefits our foundation and that is what global corporates are doing.

Another thing is to avoid lagging technologically. Any industry, any production, anything that is based on the technology of the past has to be filtered out. If we want to become a superpower, then our economy will be the most important foundation and if we want to develop it, then we have to make it capable of competing on the global level. It will be globally competitive only when its technology is ahead of its time. That is why we can't continue with outdated technology. For this, some difficulties will have to be faced. The government should try to lessen or reduce that difficulty. Such jobs, which are being done in a very traditional way, will have to be subsidised. Otherwise, it will so happen that Diwali lamps and Ganesha idols made in China will be sold here and our potters will have no work. Not all old things will survive the global competition. So, technically the old stuff has to be discarded. I must say that the digitisation programme of the government is an immense game-changer. The government is working towards making technology powerful and to go to its roots. If you digitise everything, then all your data will be on the computer. By managing data and controlling and perfecting the future of artificial intelligence, production will increase and you will be able to sell products around the world with the power of cyberspace.

And the third area, where I think, we should avoid making mistakes, is 'hard power'. I don't think I need to elaborate on hard power here. Do you know that India is now number 6 economically and has overtaken France? But in the overall power rating, India is at number 15. We lag behind smaller countries like Saudi Arabia, Israel and even Iran. This is because we have not been able to develop our hard power in that way and in that direction. Our army is vast and very professional, but we are not where we should have been. It is of great importance and you need hard power not because you have extra-territorial ambition, but because no one can dare attack you. It is this force that gives stability, an iron shield within which your economy, your industry, your human resource development, and even your democracy can survive and thrive. Without that strength, there would probably be no iron armour to protect them. For hard power, the Indian mindset has to change that has been around for centuries, i.e. we are always preparing for the wars of the past. When we started fighting, we felt that because our horses did not have stirrups, we lost the war. We just sat on blankets. Then we arranged for stirrups. When the enemy came again, he had the reins and we were again one step behind him. We were ready, but for the war that would have happened in the past. Now no war will be fought like the Second World War. Now a new type of war will be fought.

Wars are gradually becoming an ineffective and costly means to achieve political objectives. We are fulfilling the purposes of war through other means. We are rapidly moving towards a fourth-generation war. The fourth-generation war will be fought against invisible enemies. The Soviets were far ahead of the Mujahideen in terms of all powers including hard power, economic power, military power, and technical power, yet the Soviets were defeated in Afghanistan. The Vietnamese made the Americans bite the dust.

Therefore, it is not true that having advanced weapons, better communication, a bigger budget and a bigger army will lead to victory. It is not that they are not needed, but much more than that is needed and we have to think in terms of what kind of wars will take place in the future. Technological advances will be so high that wars may be contactless. Don't we need to prepare and invest heavily? There should be enormous investments for this reason so that we can achieve superior technology for warfare. I understand that the new government has tried to implement similar ideas. We have done many things. The National Security Council Secretariat has been reorganised, in which we have created a separate department only for science and technology. We have taken this step to enhance our capability of science and technology to meet the needs of the future.

Covert Warfare: Covert warfare can take many forms. If you want to influence a country so that it does what you want it to do—if you get the government of your religion formed or put your people in it, then that too is like winning a war. If you want to see what is going on in the US Government using cyber systems, you can do that, too. If such experiments are not successful today, they may be successful tomorrow. How much danger are we in? It's a new kind of warfare, in which you can create and destroy governments with the power of technology. This is the secret war. Secret warfare can be used to attack your economy, sabotage labour relations, influence your media policy, propagate disorder, your cyberspace, your entire mega data, all your information that is being gathered so that major reforms can be carried out; if they are destroyed, many Indian assets will be destroyed. There is one more thing that I think we should avoid, i.e. we should not depend on other countries. When it comes to India's independence in military equipment, whether we have a complete chain or nothing, it is the same thing. If electricity comes from the Bhakra Nangal Dam to your house and only one centimetre wire is cut in Ambala, then there will be no electricity in your house. There is nothing like 70 per cent indigenisation, 80 per cent indigenisation, 90 per cent indigenisation in defence; it has to be 100 per cent. Otherwise, we will have the gun but not the cartridge or we will have the cartridge but not the chamber; now we have to try to keep the whole system with us. Whatever we have, it should be ours. This is what the new government is doing. All the new platforms that are coming into being will have 100 per cent transfer of technology, there will be a transfer code. Now we have signed those documents, which we were denied for a long time. Whether it is the agreement with Australia or missile MJRTP, India is a part of everything. Now we have authority over it and have a legal right. If we have money, we can acquire any technology. We don't need to make a hundred things. But whatever we will make, we will make it completely here, whether it is technology, parts or anything else. This is what India should do in the future as well. Increase self-reliance and if you can excel, as we have done in many areas, whether it is Brahmos or other areas, then perhaps India will become much more self-reliant in military logistical capability.

■ India is Set to Become a Superpower: Doval ■

India has the capability to do everything on its own. Soon India is sure to become a superpower. No one in the world can stop it, except us. Perhaps we will have to work the hardest to stop this. Stop working so hard. Let us try to do something good. Forget the blame and negativity and build this country and take this message to every nook and corner of the country. For the next 10 years, India needs a strong, stable and decisive government. There should be no doubt about it. Only then will we be able to achieve our national, political, economic and strategic objectives. There should not be a manipulative government. It has to be decisive. Weak alliances will not be good for India. Democratic institutions must be strengthened at all costs. The rule of law should be followed with due diligence and devotion. False and malicious propaganda must be fought on a war footing. Don't underestimate the power of false narratives. Sardar Patel had dreamed of a great India; if you want to realise the dream of that great India, then we all have to make a united and concerted effort with our hearts and minds.

❑

19

Bangladeshi Infiltration: The Biggest Threat

Hailing from Garhwal, Doval has excellent credentials as an 'Operation Man'. He made a name for himself as a field operative in the Mizoram rebellion, where he overpowered the rebel leader Laldenga. In 1989, he led an IB team along with the Punjab Police and the National Security Guard in 'Operation Black Thunder' to flush out terrorists from the Golden Temple in Amritsar. An interview revealing his frank opinions on various issues facing the country:

Question: What are the challenges before India in matters related to internal security?

Ajit Doval: Several studies have been undertaken in India and abroad in the last decade to find out what exactly India's security vulnerabilities are. All the studies agree on one point, i.e. India's internal weaknesses are much greater than its external weaknesses. Whether you read the Group of Ministers Task Force Report, the National Security Advisery Board Report, or the US State Department assessments—all say that the internal security vulnerability is 75 to 80 per cent.

In a global context, after the Second World War, very few countries lost their territory, their constitution, and their economy due to external factors. The breakup of East Timor, Bangladesh and the Soviet Union was due to internal factors that led to civil war or the breakdown of law. India is an old civilisation, which is getting transformed into a new nation-state. It is highly exothermic. This heat is necessary because it causes strengthening.

But this process makes the fault lines fluid. India has all the fault lines—ethnic, religious, cultural, linguistic and caste-related. Synthesis is continuing, but the strengthening has not yet taken place. The transition is a difficult phase. I am hopeful that in the year 2050, the fault lines due to education, economy and development will be removed. India's internal vulnerability is also due to political factors.

The fate of political leaders lies in exploiting these fault lines, while all political leaders want to strengthen national unity. Their future lies in exploiting the fault lines. There are contradictions here. To get the votes of a particular community, they have to push in their favour. If the minority or the majority are not afraid of each other, then there will be no vote bank. So, politicians have to give voters an imaginary or real perception of fear. The genius of politics lies in exploiting fear and innovating.

But there are very positive, capable and determined people inside and outside the government, who will remove these defects.

Question: This is the wider picture. But can you tell us how you see the micro issues? Which is the most important issue for India's internal security?

Ajit Doval: I consider Bangladeshi infiltration to be the biggest internal security problem. This is the biggest issue because the government feels that it cannot do anything about it. There is no military response. Diplomatic responses have failed. Border management is not effective, and legal response is not possible as it will take 200 years to decide on 20 million illegal people. Even if you take those outsiders to the border, Bangladesh will not accept them; and even when they are accepted, they return after 15 days to a new destination in India. When an Indian court finds someone guilty as a Bangladeshi, his government escort buys him a ticket, gives him food, and takes him to the border. But in several cases, Bangladesh Rifles refuses to accept India's evidence. Bangladeshis enjoy a paid holiday in this country!

Even if he is accepted, he can come back to Dhaka on a border bus after paying touts around ₹ 3,000.

Question: Why does Bangladesh hate India?

Ajit Doval: India's problem is that if you have a support base of 20 million people who are immigrants, then how do we fight sabotage? It is difficult to infiltrate 5 terrorists or 50 sabotages or 200 persons involved in communal violence. Pakistan will never be able to send 200 people to the border at a time. 2,000 persons can enter from Bangladesh if you pay ₹ 3,000 per person. It is simply not possible to stop them.

Let me tell you about an interesting incident about a man arrested in Guwahati. His name was Salim Qari who was blind since birth. He was a resident of Muzaffarnagar in Uttar Pradesh. While living in Kupwara, Kashmir, he carried out a militant operation for nine years. He was the mastermind of many terrorist activities. He fled to Pakistan when we targeted him. After that, there was no trace of him. He was a member of an organisation that is involved in 'Bleed India' activities. Salim later surfaced in Guwahati along with five other terrorists and fortunately was arrested. You should read his revelations which were made public by the then chief minister of Assam in the state assembly.

He disclosed the number of Indian Muslims taken to Bangladesh and Pakistan. He talked about the modules they are making at various places in India. He revealed how Bangladeshis are targeted for doing their jobs in different parts of India. Many Bangladeshis are actively involved in espionage work. Modules of Lashkar-e-Taiba are also used by illegal Bangladeshis in India to do their dirty work.

Question: Is Bangladesh the next terrorist frontier?

Ajit Doval: The Tabligh-e-Jamaat meeting in Dhaka in the year 2001 was an eye-opener for India. It was the largest gathering after Hajj in Mecca. More than 40 lakh Muslims had gathered there. A large number of people from India attended. Never before had we heard so many anti-India speeches in any such gathering. Those speeches were delivered at an event that was attended by the prime minister, the chief justice, and several other top leaders of Bangladesh. The whole atmosphere that is being created there is that India is an enemy country. Jamaat-e-Islami hates India the most. Aamad is promoting Pakistan's 'Inter-Services Intelligence'. It is also a route for arms smuggling and helps in the Northeast insurgency. Bangladesh supports India's demographic invasion. This is changing the colour of many constituencies.

Later, political compulsions would prevent politicians from taking decisions in the best interest of India.

Question: In such a situation, what are the options for India?

Ajit Doval: Somebody has to be given work. Find the man and assign him the task. Ask their team to deliver. Monitor how many Bangladeshis return. Even if we get a 20 to 30 per cent return, it will have an effect. You will recall that there are over 200 constituencies across India where politicians will be tempted to decide in favour of immigrants and compromise on national security. Infiltration of Bangladeshis will lead to politics of communalism.

Question: Why is India worried about Bangladesh?

Ajit Doval: India's intelligence infrastructure should have done the job of deporting illegal migrants.

Intelligence infrastructure is a part of a larger system. No such part can overtake a larger system. Nuts and bolts cannot overtake the engine that runs the system!

Question: Why were effective measures not taken during the National Democratic Alliance regime to control the influx of Bangladeshis?

Ajit Doval: You are assuming that I do not know the evils of smoking, that's why I am smoking. But maybe I know the evils, but I still smoke. Knowledge in itself is no guarantee of action.

Question: But what did you do when you were in IB, in various senior positions?

Ajit Doval: Many steps were taken during the NDA regime, which were not strictly followed then. The identity card system was introduced. A pilot project was completed. An astronomical amount was spent on that system, which would have helped in strengthening national security. If you go to a hotel, if you fly, if you buy a house, everything that you do, you would need that I-card. It was a response to a national threat.

Then, for the first time, a task force on internal security was created and a multi-agency centre was created. For the first time, a unified national security understanding was developed.

Question: But why were you not effective on the issue of Bangladeshi infiltration?

Ajit Doval: I was part of a team that had 11 players on the field. You have to play from a certain position. The captain of the team decides on such issues. Policy execution is always a subordinate function of the policy-making function of the government.

Question: What other issues adversely affect India's internal security?

Ajit Doval: Border management is a serious problem area. The management of the Indian borders both in the north and even the coastal frontiers deserves more attention. This is being looked into, but we need more vigilance. India has more than 15,000 kilometres of land border and about 7,500 kilometres of coastline. Remember, if the border with Pakistan had been secure, there would have been no rebellion in Punjab. Kashmir's problem would have been much smaller if a substantial quantity of arms and ammunition had not crossed the border. We know for certain that 54,000 AK series rifles have been confiscated. That's why we know that most of these weapons come through the Indo-Pak border. More than 1,000 kgs of RDX seized by India means that more than 100 trucks have arrived without the goods being traced.

Imagine, since these weapons and RDX have arrived, then how many people have infiltrated India from Pakistan with this material? More than 15,000 people have gone to Pakistan for training and have returned with weapons.

In addition, we have a special area, 200 kilometres from the sea, which has great strategic and economic importance. The Indian Ocean is becoming an area of competition.

We need a national priority for internal security management and once a policy is set, we should implement it. If it is not executed, it means that India is a soft state.

Question: Apart from Bangladeshi infiltration and border management, what are the other major concerns for managers of national security?

Ajit Doval: The Naxal problem, also known as the 'Left Extremist Movement', is another extremely important issue plaguing India. This is another dangerous area for internal security.

When we talk about securing India, we ask ourselves, what are we trying to secure? When we try to fence the border, we are protecting our territorial integrity, our sovereignty. We are trying to protect ourselves from the activities of Inter-Services Intelligence. But when we deal with Maoists, we are attempting to secure our rule of law and our Constitution.

When we talk about countering Maoists, we talk about securing our system of governance. Maoists are a threat to our Constitution, the rule of law and our form of governance. They want to change rules and governments not through ballot boxes but through violence.

Question: How do we keep the youth away from Maoists?

Ajit Doval: This concern has serious implications for India's national security.

First, the vast geographical extent of Maoist influence affects 40 per cent of India. In terms of the actual operational area, it is four times more than the Punjab insurgency, Kashmir militancy and Northeast insurgency combined. Second, the response to this problem will be difficult.

What do you expect when public courts are set up in the presence of 10,000 people and death sentences are given and the Indian police don't even register an FIR? The official response of the Maoists is the trickiest part of the issue. When the Punjab problem started, the Indian Government could not cover the rural areas of Punjab even with the heavy deployment of paramilitary forces.

Only a small stretch of the valley is affected in Jammu and Kashmir, but we need five to six army corps and paramilitary forces and still, it is difficult for the police to cover the interiors of Kashmir.

The Maoist movement is in the vast hinterland of India. If a place is jointly attacked by 10,000 people and if 30 per cent of them are armed, the security personnel cannot retaliate as the resultant killings will cause maximum damage. Do you know why more than 1,000 people joined hands in the Jehanabad jailbreak? They need only 25–30 trained and skilled men to break the cordon and attack the prison. But as Charu Mazumdar said, "Every revolutionary must get his hands smeared with blood."

As is the practice in underworld gangs, when a newcomer arrives, they ask him to commit a murder so that he becomes an accused and then he will have no option but to join the gang permanently. Those who joined hands in the raids in Jehanabad jail will be with the Naxalite movement for life as they are all co-accused in the heinous crime.

More than 500 such incidents have been committed by Maoists in the last two years. Imagine how much power they have! Maoist leaders know that if they have to fight the Indian

Army, they cannot win against an 'occupied state'. If you don't have the people's 'shield', then all those 'free zones' can't remain free.

Question: Do you agree that the Maoist movement is a political movement?

Ajit Doval: It is a cent percent political movement. Maoists want to grab power through the barrel of a gun.

Question: Is this a structured movement?

Ajit Doval: It's a perfectly structured organisation. They have a politburo and a central committee. They have regional offices and now they have regional commanders. They have an army and they have commanders for soldiers.

Question: Why can't the intelligence agencies arrest them and prosecute them?

Ajit Doval: Can you do whatever you want? There is a marked difference between what you want and what you are capable of.

Question: Is India capable of controlling or taking action against the Maoists?

Ajit Doval: India can if it decides to do so.

Question: What is the major action taken by the government so far?

Ajit Doval: The government has started some welfare measures. The government is sending central soldiers if needed. A committee of chief ministers of Maoist-affected states is being formed.

There is a committee in the Home Ministry meeting periodically to discuss the Maoist problem. But so far nothing seems to be working.

The response of the government is not enough. When an incident happens, five or seven battalions of the Central Reserve Police Force are sent in, regardless of whether those soldiers make a difference or not. As the prime minister has said, we have to think out of the box. We have received conventional responses so far.

It is a completely different problem in character. It has social, security, economic and communication dimensions. I consider this a very important national issue because it is in the hinterland of India. This is the geological and forest wealth of India. All surface arteries of communication pass through it. When Punjab, Jammu and Kashmir, and the Northeast were disturbed, it did not have much impact on the rest of India. The Maoists levy tax on every truck passing through their area. The judicial system has collapsed. Rail traffic cannot run smoothly as most of the trains pass through those areas. They are collecting taxes now. They are not only allotting private land, but they are also distributing leases of government land. If you give up your judicial work, if you give up your legislative work and if you don't collect taxes, then where is the sovereignty of India? The legitimacy and credibility of the government are at stake.

Question: Where is the situation heading?

Ajit Doval: The day it is realised that this problem is very serious, it would require a national response. The first thing that should emerge is the political consensus in India.

Question: Do Maoists get the support of jihadi organisations?

Ajit Doval: Not from jihadis. But they have strategic ties. They had strategic links with the Liberation Tigers of Tamil Eelam for some sort of training.

Question: How are they funded?

Ajit Doval: The government's development fund is their main source. They snatch these funds because of poor governance. From Patwari and top government officials to local politicians, everyone remains silent.

This is not a frightening scenario, rather it is an incident that requires awareness.

They are considered neither criminals nor terrorists.

There is no accepted definition of terrorism. If they use violence to achieve their political objectives, then why do you say they are not terrorists? Terrorists are condemned because their means are unacceptable in civil society and hence their purpose is defeated.

Question: Home Minister Shivraj Patil said that Maoists are the children of our country.

Ajit Doval: Well, Dawood Ibrahim is also a child of our country. The terrorists who killed Indira Gandhi were also children of our country.

Let us understand at different levels, work at the socio-economic level, build colleges and schools, provide employment and hospitals and redress the grievances of the people. But the lack of these things does not give anyone a licence to kill innocent people.

Question: Maoists think that beyond a limit they are unable to tolerate injustice.

Ajit Doval: Yes, they can think strongly about what they do. But the Indian state cannot accept that thinking. Anyone who resorts to violence is not acceptable.

If the state tries to be soft then we should change the Constitution of India. No one has the right to kill and there should be no justification for their actions.

The main thing to decide is whether the Indian society accepts violence as a just means to achieve its political objective. If the answer is 'no' then the Maoist movement is terrorism.

If you call them black and white there will be several reactions. It will be a kind of war.

This war has to be fought and won. When I say this, I do not mean that the Maoists have no real problem or any reason. That does not mean that the government process has not failed in those parts of India.

In those parts, we have failed to govern and we have failed on the economic front. But the question is about a framework to deal with violence.

Question: In other words, does this mean that it is a civil war?

Ajit Doval: It is not a civil war right now, but it could lead to serious conflict. We have to prepare the structure. We have to persuade them to contest the elections. It is possible to explain to them. When Vinod Mishra came in after Charu Mazumdar, he built the Maoist Communist Centre and contested the elections. Some split ultra-left groups have joined the MCC in Bihar and the People's War Group in Andhra Pradesh.

Question: Don't you think that a bigger problem is that people in urban India have many more privileges, including access to technology, than people who join or support the Maoists?

Ajit Doval: You are absolutely right. The first task of the government is to reach out to the people. This work has to be done by the political leaders. We need to reach out to them and connect with them.

Question: What do you remember most about managing the Maoist issue when you were the IB chief?

Ajit Doval: At that time, the government had decided to talk to them despite some unheard voices. Peace has to be given a chance; but in conflict resolution, clarity of mind is the most important thing. It should be clearly decided who to talk to, what to offer and who can influence them the most.

Question: How well is India preparing to deal with these problems?

Ajit Doval: India has been able to tackle them fairly well. How many countries have fought so many types of terrorism for so long and with so much success?

❑

20

Be Firm in Your Decisions: Doval

Question: During the airstrike or surgical strike, you must have been in the war room, where you were probably monitoring the whole situation every single minute. So, what was going through your mind? And at any time did you have a fear or a feeling that this decision might be wrong or that you made the wrong decision? So, what was your mood at that time?

Ajit Doval: I have undertaken many operations. I cannot give the inside information about this particular operation. But I will tell you one thing—we are all humans and the human brain and human mind work in almost the same way. The difference is how you react to it. It is just like the rains. Rain falls on all of us equally; some people catch a cold, some people are fully clothed, and some have raincoats. So, when you take major decisions, when you make important decisions, there is always a sense of panic, a sense of uncertainty because you can't see the future, you can't predict the future. You only know whether the decision was right or wrong when the result is out, when everything is over. But more important is how you deal with it. How do you plan it? I can tell you that if I make a decision, I would see what could happen in the worst-case. I guess what happens when everything goes wrong and then you see what happens when everything goes wrong! Can this risk be taken? Understand that the press and media will write and talk a lot about you, but the mission will not suffer. Maybe we have to lose some lives, even then it doesn't matter. We can deal with it. The country can bear this shock. After assessing the worst-case scenario, you try to improve it. That's how I see it.

Let's say I buy a lottery ticket or let's say if I do something that goes wrong and it will cost me

₹ 500. But I will see how to reduce this expense. So, you try to make it more affordable and keep doing so until you feel that the risk is worth taking. It takes time, and preparation; sometimes our work requires technology, excellent intelligence, and much more. That's why I wanted to say that while dealing with fear if you voice that fear in clear words, you will find that the fear is not very big. It is not as big as you are worried it is. It is much less than that. Not only this, you can reduce it further with better preparation, better knowledge, better understanding and hard work. The second big thing is that for important decisions you should have a plan for an emergency, a position for retreat. Whenever you do so, things change. Now that is a new situation that you have to face and if you have to face it, then you have to make a new contingency plan for that. It could be favourable; or even unfavourable. Like the media was talking a lot during the 'Balakot operation'. This is a new situation, a favourable situation. If this is a new situation, then you have to plan as to how to deal with people's opinions or if an international issue arises, then you have to calculate it. What will be your contingency plan after the news comes out? Whatever was meant to happen has happened, favourable or unfavourable, a new situation will emerge and then you have to deal with it. That's why I think the level of fear abates considerably.

You know you have to handle it, prepare for it. You know you have the talent, knowledge, resources and everything you need. So, whatever happens, we will deal with it.

Question: Fear can be dealt with, as you said, with mental preparation and training. But sometimes you don't have options while taking decisions and then you have to make really tough decisions. When it comes to national security and you have to make a difficult decision, it can have far-reaching consequences, it can affect many generations. So, what do you keep in mind when you are making a difficult decision? Is it different from the fear of making a decision?

Ajit Doval: First of all, let us understand that we all make hundreds of decisions every day—what to wear, what to eat, what to say or buy, etc. The question is, what is it that makes a decision difficult? What are difficult decisions? Difficult decisions are those whose consequences can affect a large number of people over a long period of time. The risk is high because some of those wrong decisions can change the course of history. Say, when India got independence and states were being merged, then a decision was taken that we should go to the United Nations because the tribesmen were coming armed with weapons from the Pakistan side. Instead of directly giving them a befitting reply, we thought we should go to the United Nations. After that we came to a position where it became an international issue and we could not liberate Pakistan-occupied Kashmir. So, it was a decision that had far-reaching consequences. Even today, the problem that exists in Kashmir is because of that. Otherwise, 535 princely states were merged with India and that, too, was a princely state, which should have been merged with India. But since we decided to go to the United Nations, it became difficult for us, which was not in our national interest.

So, how do you make difficult decisions? The first thing is that your objectives should be clear like a mirror in front of you. Eliminate all adjectives and adverbs. There should be only nouns and verbs. It should be made as short and simple as possible. Don't say that we are going to fight terrorism. This is not the objective. In this case, say, we are going to destroy a person or module on a certain date. It is the purpose of that action, which is clear to you, and when it happens then do the next thing which is to speak. So, your objectives should be very well defined. Usually, we Indians get entangled in the things, thoughts, troubles, and worries of the world while not focusing on the objectives. After that, you should do an unbiased analysis of your capabilities, your circumstances, your compulsions, and available resources—whatever they may be. When I say purpose, it is very important and so is the case with me.

Whenever I make a decision, I ask myself a few questions—Am I angry? I never decide if I am angry because when you are angry you usually cannot take decisions based on facts and you do not have objectivity. Am I scared? If I am scared, my decisions won't be objective. For me, the safety of my life becomes more important. So, my decision will be influenced by whether I will come back alive or die after that. So, I say, all right, I will wait. I will decide tomorrow after I have decided what to do; if I die, I don't care, I am prepared for it. Whatever my responsibility is, which I am worried about, I have made arrangements for it. If you are angry, you feel that your personal interests are at stake, you may lose your job, or so on—people have various concerns. Don't decide at that time. Let it settle down. To be objective, you must take a decision in a completely calm state of mind, in a completely calm mood, in a completely neutral state of mind.

Then when you have defined the objectives, see what are the options with which you can achieve those objectives. Tough decisions don't have many options, yet there are choices and your experience and your knowledge make those choices the best. Then you say, I have to go from here to Connaught Place. How do you choose the best option? Every option has a cost. Every option has a timing. With every choice, there are opportunities by which they can be made. The one that suits you best is the best option, which is the most economical one and you can definitely achieve your goal. Now, there are some people who usually don't make wrong decisions but make wrong choices, wherein they say that their decision was wrong. The decision wasn't wrong, the choice you made was wrong, and why you made the wrong choice is because you didn't do the research. The research regarding your information, your experience, your database, and your interactions with people who could have helped you was not done properly. So, though you made a choice and decided to go to Connaught Place, you ended up reaching Chandni Chowk! Then you say that my two hours were wasted. The decision to go to Connaught Place was not wrong, you took the wrong route. How would you know which is wrong and right or the way? It is when you open the map. When you understand every road, every turn on the map, then you will reach via the fastest route with the least petrol and in less time. So, consider your options and prepare for them. When you have selected the option, then start preparing for it and that is the most important thing. I want to emphasise that it is most important that you do your best. Your decisions are not right or wrong. What happens is that you take a decision, but do not work in that direction and are unable to make it fruitful with complete dedication. Taking right decisions is important in life, but there is something, which is even more important, that is, implementing decisions. So, taking the right decision is not as important as making the decision right. Once you have made a decision, then you have the courage, your determination, your foresight, your spirit of tolerance, you have the ability to do it to justify that decision since you have taken it and you have taken responsibility. Well, even if a wrong decision has been made or there is a slight mistake, you can still try to correct it and for this reason, you must focus more on the action instead of changing the decisions. Once you have decided, then go for it.

Question: This question is about the way you work. You must have undertaken hundreds of operations in India or abroad and most people call you a 'solo-flyer'. So, what is it that sets Ajit Doval apart from others?

Ajit Doval: Well, it is true that I have undertaken many operations because I have been assigned those tasks throughout my life. I was very young and I don't know why it was thought that I could go on an operation. And after that, I was busy with similar things till I became the chief. But to be honest, I have never thought about whether I am any different! I think every person is different. Every creation of God is unique. How can two people or personalities be alike when two fingerprints cannot be the same? They will be different. I am different, too. But my own upbringing, education, life experiences may have brought certain characteristics. I hear such things; so, you are right that people think I am a solo- flyer. I want to work like this. Sometimes it is said in a negative way, sometimes people say it with a good intention. But there is one reason why I have been a 'solo operator'. So, I think I probably know my situation. Why put others at risk where I can take a risk? They may have been ordered to do so in such circumstances. But when I do, I do what I believe in. Let them do what they believe in. That is why I have a very strong belief or determination in what I do. I know that I am used to it. Others may have doubts and as they say in Sanskrit— *'Samshayatma Vinashyati'*, if you are in doubt you will never be successful, especially in an operation. That's why whatever I do, I never have doubts. I know that I have made a decision, worked hard, done my research, prepared myself, equipped myself, and then I will do it. Maybe some people are doing this and it is a good thing. They take it as a command, but their dedication and their faith are not of the same level. Also, I don't want other people to take risks for a task that is entirely designed by me.

Many things are said. Mr. Marwah has written a book about what happened in the Golden Temple. Around 300 terrorists had entered the temple. Then we had to carry out 'Operation Black Thunder'. At that time, someone had to go in, regardless of his appearance or identity. I was the head of the operation, so I had to do it. I knew there was little hope of survival, especially when you go for a long time and I had to go repeatedly. Others told me, "Doval sir, we will go with you." I said that no one would go with me, if someone would go with me then it would be riskier. Another thing is that if you are alone in an intelligence operation, then you are safest because no one can intercept you. Even if you get caught, your lies will be considered the truth and if you are very smart and intelligent then you can turn them around. You don't have to think about what the other man said. It's not that he's wrong, but he's different. So, they can find out the difference between the two. Well, this is a plus point of working alone. Another thing that is said about me is that the campaigns that I undertake have surprises. There is another thing that I have been working on. I never ever do anything twice. I started when I was 20 and now, I am 77. I have never repeated anything. I always like to do everything differently, as if it were the first time. Every campaign, be it big or small, happens for the first time in my life. That is why I do it with the same spirit as a child doing something for the first time because then you are not dependent on anyone and there is no prejudice. What is the guarantee that if I was lucky last time, I will be fortunate this time too! Prove your assumptions over and over again. If I made very good *biryani* yesterday, there is no guarantee that I will make it the same today. I still need to see that the chicken cooks well and the rice is better. Everything in life, every second of your life is the first second of the rest of your life. Every day of your life is the first day of the rest of your life. Start it in the same way. Then comes speed. People say that I walk very fast. I even speak very fast.

If you think that your confidential information has been leaked and your enemy has got to know about it, you have time as long as he assesses it, as long as he understands. Then if you respond quickly, you want to defeat him—in days, hours, minutes or seconds, he will reach you, but he will be two minutes late and by that time you will be gone. So, be quick to hit and quit. Don't be lethargic and be sure to keep up the pace. Of course, confidentiality is a major part of this profession. However, I have always believed that you should have the ability to always mingle and talk, but important things should be kept confidential. So, maintain extreme secrecy, which gradually becomes a way of life. You become a secretive person. That is why I understand and others also feel that there is a lot of surprise in all the operations that I have undertaken, there is speed, there is confidentiality; and don't they say that I work 'solo'?

Question: You mentioned many interesting things about speed, secrecy, etc., which are actually shaped by your mind. What kind of attitude does a person develop over a given period of time? Would you like to tell us some incidents in your life that helped you to develop this kind of attitude?

Ajit Doval: There was no incident that I created or planned to affect my attitude. The things you have planned do not affect your attitude because you have planned them. The things that affect your attitude are those that have happened and which you have not planned and they leave their mark. If

I remember, my childhood was difficult. My father was an army officer and when I was born, a child had been born in the family after 40 years. I was the only son and the others were my sisters. So, I was pampered a lot. My grandfather, my mother and the rest of the people also loved me, meaning I was mollycoddled a lot. To some extent, I was even spoiled, as it happens. So, my father sent me to a boarding school. I enrolled in military school. I was eight years old at that time. I left my home at the age of eight and joined what was then known as 'King George's Royal Indian Military College' which later became 'King George's School' and now is known as 'British School'. In this way, my life had shifted from the comfortable atmosphere of my home to the desolation of boarding school. I used to cry for hours at night because I had to sleep alone. But soon I realised that I had to live this life in my own way. You have to bear your pain, anxiety and comfort. So, I became a loner. It was good for my profession as well. But it also taught me that I would be responsible for whatever I do; that if other students beat me up, it would mean that I didn't handle them properly. That was the first incident in my life, and when I look back, I understood that if I wanted to do something, then I would have to do it alone. I have to be independent and whatever I do, I will be responsible for it. No one except me will be responsible for whatever happens to me, whether it is good or bad. I have to face the consequences. Second, the motto of that school was very strange. If they still haven't changed that, it was 'Play the Game'. Since the children used to come there at a very young age, they felt that children should be able to play sports and enhance the qualities that the sports generate in them. Every child was involved in some kind of game. I was in Chatwood House. Then the selection started. Some people got selected for football, some for hockey and some for other sports. I got selected for boxing. This is quite an interesting story. Everyone played at the school level, so I used to play, too. I was a very good boxer during my school days. One day my class teacher told me this story. He asked me, "Do you know why I chose you for boxing?" He told me that there was a unique quality in me. At that time no one knew who would be tall or short. All children were small. There must have been a difference of one inch or so. He said, "You never give up. When you are beaten, you never come out of the ring even when your blood flows; you keep fighting. It is not that you are the best fighter, but you have tremendous vitality." I will win the war not because I am the most powerful, but because I will not give up. I will wait, prepare myself and wait for many years. He said those were the qualities that a boxer should have psychologically. “According to them, you will remain in the ring till the last round, even if you lose all the rounds, even when you get beaten up, you bleed.” He said that there were boys who could fight better than me, but the moment they got hit by a punch or two, they would just call it quits. “You keep getting beaten, but you stood firm. With time, you will learn the tricks and maybe even start winning.” He said, “It is a quality—not good or bad. But remember that it is your strength if you stand tall in the face of adversity.” And that is why my tenures have been long. I went to the Northeast and stayed there for seven years. When I went to Pakistan, I stayed there for seven years. I will sustain. You can torture me or do anything, I will bear. I will tolerate injustice for a long time and will not lose my temper. At a very young age, I became independent, I got thrashed and then understood that even after being beaten, you can win.

Question: So, you made the right decision?

Ajit Doval: No, I didn't. The circumstances were such. I said that if you have taken a decision, it cannot affect your attitude. If I have decided to do something, I have prepared myself for it. If my reasoning ability is involved in this, then it will not affect it. Whatever happens in life changes your life. I didn't go to boarding school to change my attitude. But suddenly I realised that the comfort of my mother's lap was no longer there. There were many children there and when the child sees a new child, he is an enemy to him till the situation settles down. You have to beat each other to start with and everyone beats the new child who comes in. That's why you are a pillow which everybody will attack. This is the process of growing up. After some time, you also become a senior, but you do not know how it will affect you. But in the whole world, my strength, my vitality and my patience are everything. If you want, you can go to a corner and cry, run to the class teacher and tell them that you have been beaten up and tell the children not to do that. But the next day as you are walking, someone will elbow you. Somebody will do something else. Similar things will keep happening. You cannot stop the things that are happening to you from happening. What is happening to you is important in life, and more important is how you react to it. I understand that nature or circumstances are preparing me for that, not for what happens to me because it is in the hands of God, but he is preparing me for how I will deal with it if something happens to me.

Question: What you are trying to say is that it is more important to be right according to the situation than the decisions?

Ajit Doval: No. I don't think so either. It is not binary. It is not that a decision is correct or circumstantial. First of all, no one takes the wrong decision. Whether the decision is right or wrong is known only when the incident takes place. That is why when you take that decision, you feel that it is right; otherwise, you would not have taken it. Will you eat poison when you know it is poison? Let's say someone gives you candy and you eat it and it turns out to be poisonous. When the decision was taken it was right because you were not aware. So, it is wrong to say so. Second, every decision, whether right or wrong, takes into account several aspects. Circumstances is one of them. Let's say we are sitting in this room and someone enters with an AK-47. The situation here is special. In this situation, you have to make a decision. You see that this is the way and you have to go through it or break the door and get out from it. Now, this situation will not be the same when we are on the veranda. But there are eight people who have weapons. This situation would not be the same if they were on the road where you have time to pull out a gun. It is not a matter of right or wrong alone, the situation or the place matters. But your consideration of the situation is not the only aspect. Many other factors need to be considered, as I said—what is your purpose, why are you undertaking this mission, why are you doing this? Anything can happen, i.e. what do you want to achieve, what are your resources. But it has to be right or it has to be circumstantial, means that if it is circumstantial then it will not be right and if it is right then it will not be circumstantial. In this case, when you are talking about right, it is more about morality or more about value. If it is a matter of value, then there is a conflict between what you want to do and what you should do.

Question: Or what do you have to do?

Ajit Doval: No. What you should do and what you have to do—both are different. What you should do is your duty. But what you want to do is pressure. If you have to choose between what you have to do and what you are forced to do, choose the other because you have no choice. This is not a decision. It is someone else's decision. If you take out a gun and shoot at me, it is your decision. All I can do is laugh or cry. That is all I can decide. Decisions are taken only when there are alternatives. When there is a compulsion, then it is not a decision.

Question: What do you think about future wars, future terrorism? Cyber security has also become very important?

Ajit Doval: In fact, after the Second World War and the creation of weapons of mass destruction, humans are guaranteed to be wiped out from the earth if there are large wars. We have entered an era where wars are fought by other means. Conventional wars prove to be extremely costly as the damage caused by them is very high. If a large country fights a war or some large countries get involved with nuclear weapons then everything will be completely destroyed. Now, it will not be like Hiroshima or Nagasaki. The weapons of the past were nothing compared to the weapons we have today. One factor is that wars have now become extremely costly in terms of damage, but an even more important factor is that they are no longer a means to achieve political and military objectives. There is no guarantee that a country with a bigger army, more resources, more technology, bigger economic power or international alliances will win the war. A great power like the Soviet Union was defeated by the Mujahideen or America could not deal with the Vietnamese. In the battle between unequal powers, one created one's own large army so that one could win over the other. In today's war, when conventional warfare does not help you achieve your military objectives, you do not fight to kill people. You want to achieve something. They are being replaced by wars fought by other means. What did America or the

West do when Soviet troops entered Afghanistan? They had many options. They could wage war against the Soviet Union and could hurt the economy by imposing economic sanctions. They could have taken the issue to the United Nations by taking the diplomatic route. They could have imposed sanctions, but they could not do so since it was also a member of the Security Council. The people of Islamic countries asked them to start a jihad against the Soviet Army and in that jihad, it lost so much blood and was so tired that its army had to withdraw and Afghanistan came under the control of the Taliban government.

We are now looking at the modus operandi of the fourth-generation war. The fourth-generation war will be a war against the invisible enemy and the war against the invisible enemy will be won by one who sees that invisible enemy. This is the reason why intelligence has become the most important factor now. If you spot a terrorist out of 130 crore people, who looks exactly like you, dresses like you, walks like you, you will probably win; if you can't do that, you are probably going to lose. This is the reason why the code war is now on the rise. The second thing is technology. Travel has increased rapidly all over the world. Earlier, people used to operate in a limited area, now they can get anywhere in seconds. Then communication has also increased. They may keep the conversation a secret because they may find new ways to do so, such as mobile phones. When I started my career 50 years ago, there were no mobile phones, no internet, no cyberspace, which you mentioned. The entire cyber zone is a borderless zone, through which you can destroy the entire structure of the country. You can stop all its economic activities, banking activities, energy sector, aviation, communication, etc., and shut them down completely. Along with that, we are now in the stage of electronic warfare. In electronic warfare, if the plane takes off and if I know the code, I can change its direction. Even the pilot would have no control over it. So, if I crack the code, I can do anything because everything is being run electronically. Even the ejection system of the weapon system is run the same way because the communication signals are also going through the radar. If you can interrupt, change or manipulate it, then perhaps you can do all of it. Therefore, its role in the coming battles is going to increase rapidly. This is the reason why its importance is increasing now and it is necessary for us to face such challenges.

Question: So, when we are talking about technology, about the emerging technology, then I think now India is emphasising innovations, which we are also being promoted in a big way. At any point during your operations, have you used a product such as a drone, like the one shown in the movie *Uri* being used by NSA?

Ajit Doval: Movies are only movies after all. I will not say anything about them. But I will say that many techniques are used in the field of intelligence. They keep looking for technology. They try to find out what things are available or who those people are. They try to do so through sources, but they do not make them an integral part of the organisation. So, even when the technology is acquired, the people who provide that technology don't know who will actually use it, why they are using it, why they need it, whether they will use it in a particular way or make a major change in its parts, and this is necessary for the secrecy of the organisation. But that is not my job as an NSA. I am no longer involved in the work of intelligence. I left that profession long ago. I have seen and am greatly impressed by the wisdom, foresight and determination of the younger generation and also by their trust and confidence in me. Some time ago, a special group came to meet me. They told me that they wanted to make their own satellite. Google had organised an international competition. They told me that they had qualified and were shortlisted and that only ten people were finalised. They said that we could help them. There were some hurdles from both sides, but they did a fantastic job. Similarly, take IIT Madras, for example. I spoke to them and then I spoke to DRDO because they were making very good drones that could do the job of gathering intelligence. We found them very useful. So, I think that the youth have tremendous potential. I don't know how intelligence agencies can use them, but in the field of security, in the defence sector, DRDO and other areas, we are making full use of them and we should.

Question: So, we were just talking about *Uri*. Have you seen that movie? And do you break mobile phones? It has been shown several times in the movie.

Ajit Doval: I haven't seen *Uri*. I have never been to a cinema hall after joining IB. Sometimes I may have seen some movies on TV with my wife. I have never even been to a mall. That is why I have no social life. I had to avoid being seen in public and by the time I came out in the open in public life, it was too late to do the rest of the things and no, I don't break all those things (phones). More importantly, communication is the easiest way to infiltrate and penetrate the existing security area, which will put you in danger and communication is the biggest thing that gives you speed and other things. I can share a little secret. I do not use a mobile phone. I don't have a mobile phone. I do everything without it even though people ask how I do it. I know it is unsafe. Similarly, I do not even use the computer. I mean I do not use the computer for the internet. I use the computer as a typewriter. I do not correspond with anyone on the computer.

Question: You said that you do not use a cell phone, do not use a computer for communication, but you have many profiles on social media, on Twitter. What do you have to say about this? Several ideas are promoted on these fora by calling them your views.

Ajit Doval: I do not have any social media account nor did I have any account till now. All of them are either my well-wishers or are fake accounts. But I would like to tell the audience that whatever you see on Ajit Doval's Facebook account or Twitter account, there is no need to get confused by it. I don't have any such account. Maybe when I stop working for the government, then maybe I would create an account. But I don't have an account right now.

Question: But do you write articles and blogs, or don't you? People would like to know how they can know your thoughts on a particular topic.

Ajit Doval: Let me tell you that when I retired from the post of IB chief in 2005, I founded a think tank, which came to be known as 'Vivekananda International Foundation'. When I was given this responsibility in 2014, I developed it from the very beginning and now everyone knows about it. I wrote quite a bit and also gave some interviews during that time. I also delivered some lectures. A lot happened during that intervening period. Other than that, there is nothing authentic about what I have said.

Right now, I don't know as to what I know or what my thoughts are. It is not relevant at all. The views of the Government of India are important and I am a part of the views of the Government of India. I contribute, but many people like me contribute. Decisions are taken by the government and what is conveyed to the country is the decision of the government. In most of the cases, Prime Minister Modi takes decisions, and since I am his adviser and even though I advise him in the capacity of the national security adviser of the country, the decisions are his. The views of the prime minister are brought in front of the public and they should be. That is what is official. My own views don't matter.

Question: India is a country of youth. What would you like to say to the youth about how to take their future forward, how to make India more secure?

Ajit Doval: I think our youth are so well informed and so motivated that I don't need to tell them much in terms of information. They browse and know everything about where the opportunities are. But I want to tell them something about their attitudes, which can make their lives more worthwhile. We all have an identity. The smaller the identity, the smaller the person. Expand your identity. I have an identity; I am Ajit Doval. If I live as Ajit Doval, what I eat or what my hobbies are—that is all there is to it. But if I live for my family, then my identity gets bigger. When I live for my village, it gets even bigger; people know that I belong to a particular village. Some people identify themselves by caste and people say that he belongs to a particular caste. You are growing, but you are not getting a big identity. Connect your identity with your country. You will become part of a very big family. Today my identity is that of an Indian. I have no ethnic, linguistic or regional identity. Being an Indian is my identity. That's why I feel that I am as big as India. Every Indian should feel the same way. That's the way. You see that something wrong is happening in your country. If someone is tearing the railway seat or someone is creating a mess, then you feel bad. You feel that someone is defiling your country if they speak against it. I don't have much time, otherwise, I could have told you about many incidents. Once, Vivekananda was going to America from Japan by ship. He saw that an Indian, who had bought the ship ticket but had not bought a meal ticket, was being given some snacks instead of a full meal. He started cursing the Japanese saying that it was discrimination, etc. Maybe he probably did not even understand the language and that caused the dispute.

A Japanese got up and said, "Here is your food. Until the ship reaches its destination, I will not eat, rather I will give my food to you. But if you utter a single word against Japan, I will throw you out of the ship." He could give up his food but could not hear a single negative, objectionable or offensive word against his country. It is a feeling. Develop such a feeling. Be a big person, be large-hearted, think big. Rise above trivialities. Don't pursue small benefits, or small facilities. Think big. When you grow up, the whole of humanity becomes yours, like Buddha or Gandhiji. Your identity becomes bigger than just that of a human being. Our Vedas give us a greater identity than that of being just human; so, I am connected to everything that has life. Some people become so great that they think that the formless Brahma has given them everything. Whether there is life in it or not, it is part of me and I am part of it. This is *Aham Brahmasmi* or *Shivoham*. This is how you become great. Materialism, modern values make you a smaller person. In the eyes of your children, your wife, you keep shrinking. Even your parents, relatives, your society and country do not matter to you. You just think that only you matter.

So, change your attitude. Be proud to be an Indian, live for India. When you do this, you will be very happy, even if you die doing it, you will still be proud. Death will come anyway, but you will be proud of it. So, live your life well and die in a way that will be remembered.

❑

Inspirational Thoughts of Ajit Doval

1. Only a person dedicated to nationalism and nationalism is a true person; he has the ability to do something in life.
2. The feeling of nationalism should be kept above caste and religion. We can take a living example of this from a country like Israel, where nationality is paramount.
3. One whose morale is high rests only after the completion of the work.
4. The youth of India are the leaders of the country, they should never be ignored.

5. The battle continues till victory is achieved.
6. It is a matter of an immense challenge for a true patriot who cherishes the fire of patriotism within himself and passes it on to the next generation.
7. No one is richer than the one who has the conviction in the soul and faith in the heart.
8. First of all, the battle of life, the battle of conviction and the battle of faith are most challenging; by winning over them, one can win over all the future challenges.
9. The first fight of a person is with himself and within himself, who has to decide for himself whether to give to or take something from the religion, community or group to which he belongs.
10. Till we do not win, the fight will continue. With this feeling in mind, if you move towards any goal, then you will definitely achieve that goal.
11. To win any war, military force alone is not required, some victories also result from morale.
12. With strong willpower and determination, you can conquer anyone.
13. When you question your conviction and faith, there arises a situation of conflict, in which case you are deprived of your basic duty.

14. Can I do this work? Will we be able to find a way? When you go beyond all these issues and work with a positive and determined spirit, you will find both success and the way.
15. If you are determined in any battle, you can never lose that battle. This fight can be of any type.
16. The fight should continue till you reach the goal, till you find the destination and there is only one way to reach the destination—your conviction and faith in yourself.
17. Indian citizens have to continue their fight till India becomes *Vishwaguru*. This fight should be with one's own self.
18. Before fighting the internal or external problem of the country, one has to commit to himself that I will give something to this country, I will do something for this country.
19. We take cultural education, food, clothes, etc., from this country, but have we ever taken a pledge that we will give something to the country?
20. Being capable, powerful and tough does not mean that you should turn away from patriotism, but you can discharge your duties for the country from which you have got everything.

21. The fight for patriotism is beyond economic prosperity or poverty, in which there is no place for profit or loss.

22. After being prosperous, we should try to take our country's honour, culture, and community to new heights so that future generations can be proud of our country.

23. History is the biggest court in the world. History has been on the side of those who have been powerful, who have never supported justice and innocent people. The history of India points in this direction. Hence we have to become strong, we have to be robust to protect ourselves.

24. Justice has its own importance, but where there is talk of supremacy, it is necessary to be powerful. Behind the idea of India becoming a religious leader, there is a necessity to be powerful.

25. India also has manpower, money power, and technological power, using which we can write a new history.

26. The compassionate nature of India has always boosted the morale of the enemies. So, it is necessary to show our power to them.

27. Forget what happened yesterday and prepare for tomorrow by learning lessons from it. It

is not necessary that the next test will be tomorrow itself, but you should be ready for it.

28. The method of war changes according to time. With this changing method, we need to do our best.

29. India has not lost to foreigners as much as it has lost to its own people. India has been defeated only by Indians.

30. In the present time, the one who has the courage to fight the battle with patience will be victorious; for this, we have to be strong.

31. Pakistan poses many threats, but if it starts a war, the country of Pakistan will disappear from the map. India will still be there, but Pakistan will not remain.

32. Our own people harm the nation for their selfishness and happiness. To avoid this, it is necessary to be aware and powerful. Only the people and youth power can do this work.

33. If we make our faith stronger then no one can stop us from becoming a world power. We have all the resources we need to become the foremost power in the world.

34. We have the best resources in the world—scientists, education, technology etc., which can make us the foremost power.

35. Wherever there is danger, we will strike there. To protect the country, we cannot only go to the border, but we can also go beyond the border. This is New India, which thinks differently. History has been a witness that India does not strike first.

36. Military powers protect the state, but the security of the nation is built by the ascetics here, who have sacrificed their lives for the sake of the nation since time immemorial.

37. We fight war, not for our selfishness, but for the highest good no matter who owns the land.

38. Efforts were always made to erase the history of India. It is written in history that there was nothing in India; some people came here from Arabia, some came from Central Asia and developed their own cultures. So, we have to guard against such conspirators.

❑

References

1. 'How PM Modi, Ajit Doval and Army Chief Planned Covert Attacks Against Terrorists,' *The Economic Times.*
2. 'Possibility of Ajit Doval going to China: The famous 'Doval theory' of the NSA and breaking India's stand on Beijing', *Firstpost.*
3. 'Ajit Doval Myanmar Operations...,' India TV News (India TV).
4. ' Ajit Doval's Power Theory', *Firstpost.*
5. 'Ajit Doval: The most powerful person in India after PM Modi', *The Economic Times.*
6. 'Warm welcome to Indian nurses released in Iraq,' BBC News.
7. 'Riot situation under control in Northeast Delhi', livemint.com.
8. 'NSA Ajit Doval has a four-point mantra for success', *Hindustan Times.*

9. 'Myanmar handed over 22 Northeast rebels wanted in India after NSA Ajit Doval's intervention', Zee News.

10. 'NSA Ajit Doval to head the new Strategic Policy Group set up to assist the National Security Council', India TV.

11. 'NSA Ajit Doval underlines the use of power—India must stop punching below its weight', *The Indian Express.*

12. 'NSA Ajit Doval and General Dalbir Singh planned a retaliatory action against the terrorists,' *The Times of India.*

13. 'NSA Doval on a secret mission in Iraq', *The Hindu.*

14. 'NSA Doval's strategy of 'double squeeze' will never succeed—Pak', *The Times of India.*

15. 'Amity Award', alumni.amity.edu.

16. 'Ajit Doval who carried out surgical strikes across the LoC', India.com

17. 'How Ajit Doval suppressed the riots in Kerala in 1972', *The Week.*

18. 'Colleges, universities have the responsibility of imparting skills to students—Ajit Doval', *India Today.*

19. 'The Inside Story of How India Succeeded in the Doklam Border Standoff with China', *India Today*.

20. 'The greatest among spies—Ajit Doval is the new National Security Adviser', *Hindustan Times*.

21. 'James Bond: How 'Indian James Bond' Ajit Doval managed the riot-hit Thalasseri', *The Times of India*.

22. 'Doklam standoff: Ajit Doval proved that a diplomat is not needed to solve the international crisis,' *Firstpost*.

23. 'Doval laments the poor pace of development and development of Uttarakhand', *The Pioneer*.

24. 'The Brain Behind Modi Sarkar', tehelka.com

25. 'India's 'human capital' can compete with China's 'rare mineral wealth'—NSA Ajit Doval', *The New Indian Express*.

26. 'Myanmar Operation: 70 Commandos Completed the Job in 40 Minutes', *The Economic Times*.

27. 'Myanmar Army handed over 22 North-eastern rebels', *Hindustan Times*.

28. 'India's aggressive stand on the border is the brainchild of NSA Ajit Doval,' *The Economic Times.*

29. 'The Return of Superspy,' *The New Indian Express.*

30. https://navbharattimes.indiatimes.com›

31. https://www.aajtak.in› india › story

32. https://www.amarujala.com› Jammu

33. https://www.bhaskar.com› news› ns...

34. https://www.jagran.com› news› nati...

35. https://www.prabhatkhabar.com› national

36. 'Bangladeshi infiltration is the biggest threat', Rediff.com

❑